Canons Of The Second Council Of Orange

F. H. Woods

CANONS

OF THE

Second Council of Orange,

A.D. 529.

TEXT, WITH AN INTRODUCTION,
TRANSLATION, AND NOTES.

.

BY THE

REV. F. H. WOODS, B.D.,

FELLOW OF ST. JOHN'S COLLEGE, OXFORD.

Oxford:
JAMES THORNTON, HIGH STREET.
MDCCCLXXXII.

PREFACE.

THIS little work is primarily intended as an assistance
to those students who are reading the subject of Grace
for their examination in the Theological School at
Oxford; but it is thought that it may be useful also for
Candidates for Holy Orders, and others who are desirous
of mastering the opinions of the Church on this
important subject. In preparing the work, I have to
acknowledge my obligations to Dr. Bright's "Anti-Pelagian
Treatises," the introduction to which book furnished
me with one or two valuable hints; but in the main I
have derived my information from an independent study
of S. Augustine's works. I have derived very much
assistance in doing so from the excellent arrangement
and invaluable Index of the Benedictine Edition of
that Father. My reading, if it has done nothing else,
has at least convinced me that no adequate knowledge

of S. Augustine's opinions can be obtained except by a
study of the writer's actual works at first hand : and it
is hoped that this little book may lead others to gain
for themselves, by such study, a much more complete
and clear view than can be got by only reading through
the quotations of the Father which are here made.   Any
other works which I have consulted will be found referred
to in the foot-notes.   The quotations from S. Augustine
and Prosper are from the Benedictine edition.   The
references are made to the same edition.   The chapters
are added in brackets for the convenience of reference.

S. JOHN'S COLL, OXFORD,
    Whit-Tuesday, 1882.

INTRODUCTION.

———•◦◦•———

THE Second Council of Orange has one peculiar feature,
that it passed no original canons of its own. The object
with which the Council met, as the Preface states, was
to examine and ratify certain Articles or *Capitula*, sent
by Felix IV., bishop of Rome. This object it literally
fulfilled, adding probably nothing whatever, except the
Preface or Preamble just alluded to, and a concluding
paragraph explaining why it was that certain of the
illustrious laity had been invited to sign, as well as the
thirteen bishops. This was also an unusual step, though
not without precedent in the history of Church Councils.

These Articles, with the exception of Art. X., were
borrowed almost verbatim from two writers, viz., Prosper,
probably a layman of Aquitaine, and Gennadius, a
presbyter of Marseilles.

For an account of the former of these, and the part he
played as an opponent of Pelagian opinions, the reader
should by all means consult the Introduction to Dr.
Bright's " Anti-Pelagian Treatises." [1]

Of Gennadius nothing is known, except what we may
gather from the two works he has left us. The first, *De*

———

[1] Pp. lv.-lxi.

2

Scriptoribus ecclesiasticis, is merely an imitation and con-tinuation of the similar work of S. Jerome, the second, *Liber de Ecclesiasticis Dogmatibus*, written probably 492–94, is that from which the quotations in these Articles are made. It is a kind of summary of the writer's own faith and opinions on matters of doctrine and various religious questions. On essentials of Christian faith, the writer is in form very dogmatic, and for the most part rigidly orthodox; but on other subjects he showed himself to be a man of independent views. Thus he candidly confessed that he did not believe that the present world would be hereafter literally destroyed by fire, but only renovated.[1] On the subject of the Holy Communion, he recommended in most cases a weekly, but spoke doubtfully of the value of a daily, reception.[2] On the doctrine of grace, with which we are chiefly concerned, we find the same out-spoken candour. While he strongly insisted on the necessity of preventing grace (See Articles I.–VIII.), he condemns in the most unqualified terms the doctrine of a predestined Reprobation (see last paragraph but one of the acts of the Council); and in so doing he tacitly condemns S. Augustine himself.[3] Partly on this account, and partly on account of his depreciation of S. Augustine and Prosper, and his approbation of Faustus in the *De Viris Illustribus*, he is sometimes charged with being a semi-Pelagian. But such a charge would seem to be amply refuted by his own language in Arts. I.–VIII., and some have in consequence regarded his accounts of these people as spurious.[4] It is possible that Gennadius,

---

[1] See Lib. de Eccles. Dogm., lxx.   [2] Ibid. liii.
[3] See notes on this passage below pp. 46, 47.
[4] See Article on Gennadius, in Smith's Dict. of Eccles. Biogr.

without belonging definitely to the semi-Pelagian party, may have partially come under the influence of the semi-Pelagian Cassian, who was himself a monk of Marseilles.

The *Liber de Eccles. Dogm.* of Gennadius was, as he himself says in the account of himself at the close of his other work, sent by himself to Pope Gelasius, and hence passed into the hands of Felix, his successor, who transmitted it to the Council. If it were clear that Gennadius was a semi-Pelagian, the acts of the Council would represent a curious phenomenon, viz., a combination in one set of Articles of the statements of two writers of different and more or less directly antagonistic schools on the same subject, without the church either then or since having discovered any discrepancy between the two.

The quotations made from Gennadius only in the acts of the Council comprise Articles I.–VIII., and the paragraphs which follow Article XXV. The rest, with the exception of Article X., are all quoted from Prosper's *Liber Sententiarum.* But this work was a collection of extracts taken almost entirely (sometimes it is true, with slight alterations) from S. Augustine, and there are only three of them quoted in the acts, viz., Articles IX., XII., and XIV., which were not so derived. And the two last even of these appear to be adaptations of S. Augustine's language.[1] Three of the Articles quoted from Prosper, viz., XIII., XIX., and XXI., had been already quoted by Gennadius, and if we can trust our MSS., they would seem to have been taken verbally from that source, for the text will be found to agree with Gennadius rather than Prosper.[2]

---

[1] See notes on Arts. XII., XIV.
[2] See notes on Arts. XIII., XIX., XXI.

Thus the Articles of this Council fall mainly under three distinct heads—

(1) Arts. I.–VIII. A condemnation of semi-Pelagian opinions taken consecutively from Gennadius.

(2) IX., and XI.–XXV. Selections from Prosper's Sentences (quoted for the most part from S. Augustine) refuting various points in Pelagian doctrines, and arranged not on any doctrinal principle, but in the order in which they occurred in Prosper, but not consecutive.

(3) A general summary of the Catholic doctrine as opposed to Pelagian and semi-Pelagian views, taken consecutively from Gennadius.

The order in the second of these divisions is purely accidental. Prosper himself makes the quotations in the order in which they occurred in the books of S. Augustine he quotes. To attempt therefore to discover any doctrinal method in their arrangement must be a useless waste of labour.

Before studying in detail the language of these Articles it is important that the reader should thoroughly understand the main points at issue in the Pelagian controversy. He will then be able to see readily and clearly the bearing of smaller questions on those which may be considered fundamental. In order to do this he should first endeavour to acquaint himself with the doctrines of either party considered as a whole, and then compare their respective views in detail, and so get to understand the several points on which they differed from each other. We here give a short summary of the views of either party, which the reader should fill up from his own reading.

Following what we may call the historical order, we may divide the subject into four main divisions according as the questions affected : (1) the nature of man ; (2) sin ; (3) grace ; (4) good works.

On these four heads the views of Pelagius [1] may be described as follows—

(1) Human nature, consisting of a mortal body [2] and an immortal soul, is acknowledged in both its parts to be the creation of God, made for the highest purposes, and potentially at least good. Man thus constituted had the alternative of good and evil offered to him, with the free power of choosing either. This last is called in theological language *liberum arbitrium.* Adam as a fact chose the evil and so sinned.

(2) Sins must be regarded either as wrong actions done, or good actions omitted. They have in no sense an essential existence, and cannot therefore inherently belong to human nature, so as to affect it as a disease.[3] Adam's sin cannot therefore have produced any real effect on human nature. Men are still in a similar position to Adam, and endowed with a nature precisely similar both in body and soul. They have the same free choice between good and evil, and if they sin, they are merely following the bad example set them by Adam.[4]

(3) In order to attain to holiness, and obtain everlasting life, man needs God's help and grace in many ways.

(*a*) It is by God's goodness and power alone that man receives forgiveness for past sins.[5]

(*b*) He has a nature endowed with an inherent power

---

[1] Some of these opinions were disclaimed by Pelagius (see De Gest. Pel., passim), but, in spite of his quibbles, they may be considered a fair representation of the views held at least by his party.

[2] De Gest. Pel. (xi.) § 23.   [3] De Nat. et Grat. (xix.) § 21.

[4] De Pecc. Mer. I. (ix.) § 9.

[5] De Nat. et Grat. (xxxiv.) § 39.

of doing good (*inseparabilis possibilitas naturæ*)[1]: but this nature thus endowed is itself the gift of God, because He made it.

(*c*) He has had from various times revelations from God, especially those known as the law given on Sinai, and the gospel given by Christ. These teach man what he ought to do.[2]

(*d*) The fact that he has the choice of obeying the law thus revealed is part of God's constitution. This free-choice is therefore also a gift of God.[3]

(4) Man may, and indeed must, obtain holiness, by using all these gifts of God, and by them doing good works. Such works are the condition and ground of obtaining acceptance with God, who, being just and holy, rewards us if we do good works pleasing to Him, and punishes us if we do the contrary. Good works therefore merit God's grace (so understood) and in the end eternal life.[4] Those most insisted on are the entire renunciation of riches.[5]

There were two other doctrines closely connected and generally held with these—

(5) That as human nature was in itself sinless, it was absurd to baptize infants who had committed no actual sin, and were therefore saved if they died.[6]

(6) That it was quite possible, by the help of God's revelation without and his own natural power within, for man to live a perfectly sinless life, and several have actually done so.[7] It should be observed that, according

---

[1] De Nat. et Grat. (l.) § 58.   [2] De Spir. et Lit. (ii.) § 4.
[3] De Spir. et Lit. (xxxiv.) § 60.
[4] De Gest. Pel. (xiv.) § 33.   [5] Ibid (xi.) § 24.
[6] Aug. contr. d. Ep. Pel. I. (xxii.) § 40.
[7] De Nat. et Grat. (vii.) § 8 ; (xxxvi.) § 42, &c.

to Pelagius' view, a very large number of small sins, such especially as arise from ignorance or forgetfulness, were regarded as inevitable, and therefore, not being subject to his free-choice, as in reality no sins at all.[1]

Following the same method of arrangement, we may describe the corresponding tenets of S. Augustine almost in his own words as follows—

(1) Both parts of human nature, *i.e.*, body and soul, were made by God out of nothing. Both were originally immortal. Adam therefore, had he not sinned, would have continued to have lived on for ever. Man was endowed not merely with a bare *liberum arbitrium*, but with a goodwill (*bona voluntas*), *i.e.*, a definite love of good implied in the very idea of rectitude[2]; but even in this condition of integrity he needed God's grace to keep him from sin.[3]

(2) Sin, though not in itself having an essential existence, was able to and did affect the nature of man both in body and soul, which are substances, much as hunger or disease, which are equally without essential existence, weaken or impair the body.[4] Man's whole nature was thus by Adam's transgression "changed for the worse."[5] The *bona voluntas* was entirely lost, and his choice was no longer properly free, but inclined to evil.[6] This change affected the nature not only of Adam himself, but of all those who are descended from him, and so derive from him not only their body, but also probably

[1] De Nat. et Grat. (xii.) § 13.
[2] Aug. De Civ. Dei, XIV. xi. 1.
[3] See notes on Art. XIX.   [4] De Nat. et Grat. (xx.) § 22.
[5] See notes on Arts. I., II.   [6] See notes on Art. XIII.

their soul,[1] just in the same way as bodily diseases are sometimes inherited.

(3) The kinds of Divine grace acknowledged by Pelagius are inadequate to produce a condition of *justitia* or holiness in man.

(*a*) Forgiveness alone is not enough. It can only have a remedial effect on the past. It cannot supply strength for the future.[2]

(*b*) Nature is not enough, especially now that man has lost his original natural power. He wants, therefore, a supernatural power to restore nature, and enable him to combat with sin.[3]

(*c*) Revelations from God, in whatever form, have of themselves no power to give man the inward moral and spiritual strength he needs. They are but preparatory to grace. The only moving power they can have is terror ; but if they compel men to do right from fear of punishment, the motive is wrong, and the outwardly right actions are sins in the sight of God who sees the heart.[4] The law shows man what is right and what is wrong, but does not give him the power of obedience. Practically it frequently aggravates the evil. The rebellious spirit in man often sins all the more grievously because he cannot bear the restraint the law imposes upon him, just as the river dashes with greater violence over the barriers placed across it.[5]

(*d*) Man's choice is no longer free. If it is free in any

---

[1] See notes on Art. I.
[2] De Nat. et Grat. (xxvi.) § 29.
[3] De Spir. et Lit. (xxvii.) § 47.   De Nat. et Grat. (iii.) § 3.
[4] De Spir. et Lit. (viii.) §§ 13, 14.
[5] De Spir. et Lit. (iv.) § 6.

sense, it is only free to do evil, not to do good.[1] In either case it does not of itself constitute a moving power.

(4) Man therefore, in order to reach the desired state, and obtain eternal life, needs the special grace of God at all times, and no single good action can be done without the special help of God.[2] Good works are therefore the works of God working with us and in us,[3] and as such only can merit a reward.[4] It is the grace of God which first moves a man to seek for more grace from Him, and gives him the first beginnings of faith.[5] By the grace of God he is reborn in Baptism.[6] By the grace of God through the Holy Spirit is infused charity, by which he loves God and does what pleases Him.[7] By the grace of God he perseveres unto the end, until he reaches perfection.[8]

(5) On the first of the two remaining doctrines S. Augustine urges most emphatically and repeatedly that infants being born in sin require the Regeneration of Baptism, and cannot otherwise be saved.[9] He even argues that they are not only condemned, but justly condemned, on the grounds that sin as such deserves God's condemnation.[10] In one passage, however, he considers that God may grant them a far milder condemnation than wilful and deliberate sinners.[11]

(6) On the last point S. Augustine wavered consider-

---

[1] See notes on Art. XIII. [2] De Gest Pel. (xiv.) §§ 30, 31.
[3] See note on Arts. IX., XX. [4] See notes on Art. XVIII.
[5] See note on Art. V. [6] De Gest. Pel. (xii.) § 28.
[7] De Spir. et Lit. (iii.) § 5, &c. [8] See notes on Art. X.
[9] De Nat. et Grat. (viii.) § 9. [10] Ibid. (iv.) § 4.
[11] De Pecc. Mer. I. (xvi.) § 21. (Quoted by Dr. Bright, Anti-Pel. Treat. xiv., Note 4.)

ably. At first, on theological grounds, he was ready
sometimes to admit the possibility of being without sin
by the special power and grace of God [1] ; but he usually
modified this by asserting that no man had actually lived
here without sin, and relegating the sinless state to
man's condition hereafter.[2] He is inclined, however, in
one passage to make a single exception in the case of the
Virgin Mary.[3] In his treatise, *De Dono Perseverantiæ*,[4]
he even goes so far as to speak of the doctrine of human
sinlessness as one of the three cardinal errors of the
Pelagians; but perhaps he intended to refer only to
sinlessness deemed possible without Divine grace.

Later on the main subject of the controversy changed,
or rather the controversy was more or less restricted to a
single topic, viz., the necessity of preventing grace,
which was denied by the more moderate semi-Pelagian
party. The quotations from Gennadius (Articles I.–VIII.)
are entirely concerned with this subject. They reiterate
in a variety of ways the doctrine that man cannot himself
initiate the moral and spiritual work which results in
Regeneration, but that it depends upon God. The remaining Articles treat of this and also the other parts of
the wider subject as, especially, the need of co-operating
grace, by which alone man can persevere.

If we except the short passage bearing upon Predestination, the Articles of the Council can certainly claim to
represent the views of S. Augustine. As we have seen,
the larger number of them (XI. & XV.–XXV.) are actually
though indirectly quoted almost verbally from his writings.

---

[1] De Spir. et Lit. (i.–v.), §§ 1–7, &c.
[2] De Nat. et Grat (lx.), § 70, &c.
[3] Ibid. xxxvi., § 42.   [4] De Don. Pers. (ii.) § 4.

The first eight are so like S. Augustine's teaching that there is hardly a phrase for which we cannot find an equivalent in his works. They show that Gennadius, their author, was a man who had carefully studied and caught the spirit of the champion for Divine grace. Similarly, Articles IX., X., XII., XIV., exactly represent, though in somewhat different language, S. Augustine's teaching on the same topics.

It has sometimes been maintained, as by Milman,[1] that we have also a distinct departure from, or at least a modification of, the Augustinian theology in the insertion, as it is implied, by the Western Church of outward means of grace, such as Baptism, which narrowed the sphere of God's action to the limits of the outward and visible Church, so that while it expressly condemned semi-Pelagianism it really introduced semi-Pelagian ideas. Whether this can or cannot be fairly considered a human limitation of Divine power need not be discussed here; but it is only fair to recognise the fact that the limitation itself was repeatedly recognised by S. Augustine, who spoke sometimes in the most uncompromising manner of those who were without the reach of outward means of grace.[2] At the same time it must be confessed that by the adoption of Gennadius's alteration of S. Augustine's language in Art. XIII., and of Gennadius's own language on the connection of preventing grace with Baptism in Art. V. and in the concluding paragraph, the Council did undoubtedly give a distinct prominence to Baptism as the outward means of electing grace.

The Augustinian character of the Articles as a whole

---

[1] Hist. of Lat. Christ., Bk. ii. ch. ii.
[2] See, *e.g.*, De Nat. et. Grat. (iv.) § 4 ; (ix.) § 10.

can only be understood and appreciated by comparing the language of the Articles with that of the great father himself. And the student is recommended to make a careful study of the quotations given in full in the notes for this purpose from S. Augustine's works.

CANONS OF THE
SECOND COUNCIL OF ORANGE.

CONCILIUM ARAUSICANUM SECUNDUM.

CONSTITUTIO EPISCOPORUM IN CIVITATE ARAUSICANA, DE GRATIA ET LIBERO ARBITRIO.

In dedicatione basilicæ a Liberio patricio constructæ
celebratum, quinto nonas Julias, Decio Juniore,
viro clarissimo, consule ; id est, anno
Christi DXXIX. Felicis IV.
Papæ anno tertio.

PRÆFATIO.

Cum ad dedicationem basilicæ, quam illustrissimus
Præfectus et Patricius filius noster Liberius in Arausica
civitate fidelissima devotione construxit, Deo propi-
tiante, et ipso invitante, convenissemus, et de rebus quæ
ad ecclesiasticam regulam pertinent inter nos spiritalis
fuisset oborta collatio, pervenit ad nos esse aliquos qui
de gratia et libero arbitrio per simplicitatem minus caute,
et non secundum fidei Catholicæ regulam, sentire velint.
Unde id nobis, secundum admonitionem et auctoritatem
Sedis Apostolicæ, justum ac rationabile visum est, ut
pauca capitula ab Apostolica nobis Sede transmissa, quæ
ab antiquis[1] patribus de sanctarum Scripturarum volumi-
nibus in hac præcipue causa collecta sunt, ad docendos
eos qui aliter quam oportet sentiunt, ab omnibus ob-

---

[1] The reference is undoubtedly mainly to S. Augustine, whose
language actually is incorporated for the most part in Arts. XI.–XXV.
What follows must be understood as meaning that the tenour of the
language was derived from Holy Scripture. At same time these
Articles actually contain many scriptural quotations. Prosper is
also probably referred to. The statement is evidently taken from

THE SECOND COUNCIL OF ORANGE.

WHAT WAS DECIDED BY THE BISHOPS IN THE TOWN OF
ORANGE CONCERNING GRACE AND FREE-WILL.

Held at the dedication of the Church built by Liberius the
patrician, on the third day of July, in the consulship
of the most illustrious Decius Junior, *i.e.*, in
the year of Christ 529, in the third
year of Pope Felix IV.

PREFACE.

When, by the mercy and at the call of God, we had
assembled to the dedication of the church which the
most illustrious prefect and patrician, our son Liberius,
built out of devout piety in the town of Orange, and a
spiritual discussion had arisen among us concerning the
things which belong to the rule of the Church, it came to
our hearing that there were some who were inclined in
their simplicity to hold too careless opinions, and not in
accordance with the rule of the Catholic faith, concerning
grace and free-will. Wherefore it seemed to us right and
reasonable, with the advice and sanction of the Apostolic
See, that we should publish for all to hold, and subscribe
our signatures to, a few articles sent to us by the Apostolic
See which were collected, on this subject especially, from

---

the first sentences of the concluding paragraphs from Gennadius
(see p. 44). The Council do not seem to have been acquainted with
the Liber de Eccles. Dogm., and very probably thought that the
extracts from that work sent them by Felix were really collected by
him from some earlier fathers.

servanda proferre, et manibus nostris subscribere debere-
mus; quibus lectis, qui hucusque non sicut oportebat
de gratia et libero arbitrio credidit, ad ea quæ fidei
Catholicæ conveniunt animum suum inclinare non
differat.

CAPITULA.

I. Quod per peccatum Adæ non solum corpus, sed
anima etiam læsa fuerit.

[1] Si quis per offensam prævaricationis Adæ non totum,
id est secundum corpus et animam, in deterius dicit
hominem commutatum, sed animæ [2] libertate illæsa
durante corpus tantummodo corruptioni credit obnox-
ium ; Pelagii errore deceptus adversatur Scripturæ
dicenti: [3] *Anima quæ peccaverit ipsa morietur ;* et: [4] *Nescitis*

---

[1] From Gennadius, Lib. de Eccles. Dogm. § 38. The question of
original sin was very closely connected with certain psychological
questions concerning the origin of the human soul.   The two common views on this subject held in early Christian times are known
respectively as the *creatianist* and the *traducianist*.   According to
the first of these, the soul of each man is separately created by God.
According to the second, it is derived like the body from his
parents.   In addition to these were views having more or less of
a pantheistic character ; such as that of Origen, that all souls
had an existence from eternity ; or that again of the Manichæans,
that souls belonged to the great Divine hierarchy.   An inter-
mediate opinion between this and *creatianism* was held by a certain Vincentius Victor, who had been a Donatist, and had only
lately been converted to the Church, when S. Augustine wrote the
treatise De Animâ et ejus Origine.   Victor maintained that souls
were made by God out of Himself, and could only be the subject of
original sin from their contact with sinful flesh.   S. Augustine
argues against this view on the grounds that it is inconsistent with
God's justice for Him to condemn innocent souls to a state of union
with sinful nature, and so make them liable to its punishment.   For
the same reason he was inclined to reject the *creatianist* view, and

the volumes of the Holy Scriptures by the early Fathers to teach those who hold heterodox opinions. Having read these, let him who has not hitherto believed what he ought concerning grace and freewill without delay turn his mind to what accords with the Catholic faith.

ARTICLES.

I. That not the body only, but the soul also was injured by the sin of Adam.

If any one denies that the whole of human nature, *i.e.*, in body and soul, was changed for the worse by the offence of Adam's transgressions, but believes that while the liberty of the soul remained uninjured, the body only became liable to corruption, he is deceived by the error of Pelagius, and contradicts the Scripture which says, " the

---

adopt the *traducianist*. He expresses himself, however, with great caution : *Quid si ergo sic etiam anima et spiritus hominis et a Deo datur, quamdiu datur ; et tamen ex propagine sui generis ? Quod ego nec defendo, nec refello ; i.e.*, " Is it not possible that the soul and spirit of man, though always the gift of God, are yet given by the propagation of their own kind. An opinion which I neither defend nor refute ? " De An. et Orig. I. (xvi.) § 26. See also De Orig. An. (Ep. clxvi.) (iv.) § 10, &c. On the other hand, Gennadius himself adopted definitely the *creatianist* view. See Lib. de Eccles. Dogm. xiv.

² On the opinion that original sin involved the loss of true liberty, see below on Art. XIII.

³ The argument is curious. The word *nephesh*—of which *anima* is a translation—is used in this connection, as frequently in the Old Testament, as equivalent to "person ;" as in Gen. xii. 5 : "The souls that they had gotten in Haran." It is never used of the highest part of man's nature, which is *ruach*, and is even used of a " dead person " in Numb. vi. 6.

⁴ The last two quotations are made to prove the general depravity of the human race, which was practically denied by those who, like Victor, limited the effects of inherited sin to the body.

*quoniam * cui exhibetis vos servos ad obediendum, servi estis ejus * cui obeditis ?* et : *A quo quis superatur, ejus † et servus addicitur.*

II. Quod peccatum Adæ non ipsi solum nocuit, sed ad posteros quoque transiit.

5 Si quis soli Adæ prævaricationem suam, non et * ejus propagini asserit nocuisse, aut certe mortem tantum corporis, quæ pœna peccati est, non autem et peccatum, quod mors est animæ, per unum hominem in omne genus humanum transiisse testatur; injustitiam Deo dabit, contradicens Apostolo dicenti : *Per unum hominem peccatum intravit in mundum et per peccatum mors, et ita in omnes homines * mors pertransiit, in quo omnes peccaverunt.*

III. Quod gratia Dei non ad invocationem detur, sed ipsa faciat ut invocetur.

6 Si quis * ad invocationem humanam gratiam Dei dicit posse conferri, non autem ipsam gratiam facere ut invocetur a nobis, contradicit Isaiæ prophetæ, vel Apostolo idem dicanti : *Inventus sum a non quærentibus me ; palam apparui his qui me non interrogabant.*

---

5 From Gennadius, ibid. § 39. This Article is closely connected with the last. To limit inherited sin to the body is virtually to deny its existence. It is to make it inherited punishment, and involves injustice on the part of God, who, according to this view, punishes men for sins which belong not to themselves, but to Adam. Gennadius probably derived it from S. Aug. c. d. Ep. Pel. IV. (iv.) § 6: *Sed Pelagiani quomodo dicunt solam mortem ad nos transisse per Adam ? Si enim propterea morimur, quia ille mortuus est ; ille autem mortuus est, quia peccavit ; pœnam dicunt transire sine culpa,*

soul which has sinned itself shall die," and " Do ye not know that to whom ye show yourselves slaves to obey, his slaves ye are to whom ye obey?" and, "By whom any one is overcome, his slave he is also made?"

II. That the sin of Adam did not hurt himself only, but passed on to his descendants also.

If any one asserts that Adam's transgressions hurt himself alone, and not also his progeny, or declares that at any rate only bodily death, which is the punishment of sin, and not sin also, which is the death of the soul, by one man passed on all the human race, he will be ascribing injustice to God, and contradicting the Apostle who says, " By one man *sin* entered into the world, and death by sin ; and so death passed upon all men, because all have sinned."

III. That the grace of God is not given at man's call, but itself makes man call for it.

If any one says that the grace of God can be conferred at man's call, and not rather that grace itself makes us call for it, he contradicts the prophet Isaiah, or the Apostle who quotes his words, " I was found of those who were not seeking me ; I appeared openly to those who were not asking for me."

---

et innocentes parvulos injusto judicio puniri trahendo mortem sine meritis mortis.

 [6] From Gennadius, ibid. § 40. That the grace of God must precede prayer is frequently insisted upon by S. Augustine. Gennadius may have had in his mind, S. Aug. Enarr. in Psalm cxiv. § 5, in which, commenting on the words *Misericors Dominus et justus, et Deus noster miseretur,* he says, *Quis enim eum invocavit, nisi quem ipse prior vocavit.* See below on Article VI.

IV. Quod Deus, ut a peccato purgemur, voluntatem
    nostram non expectet, sed præparet.

7 Si quis, ut a peccato purgemur, voluntatem nostram
Deum exspectare contendit, non autem ut etiam purgari
velimus, per Sancti Spiritus infusionem et operationem
in * nos fieri confitetur; resistit ipsi Spiritui Sancto per
Salomonem dicenti: *Præparatur voluntas a Domino*, et
Apostolo salubriter prædicanti: *Deus est qui operatur in
vobis et velle et perficere pro bona voluntate.*

V. Quod initium fidei non ex nobis, sed ex gratia Dei
   sit.

8 Si quis, sicut augmentum, ita etiam initium fidei,
ipsumque credulitatis affectum, quo in eum credimus qui
justificat9 impium et ad *regenerationem sacri baptismatis
pervenimus, non per gratiæ donum, id est per inspirationem Spiritus Sancti corrigentem voluntatem nostram
ab infidelitate ad fidem, ab impietate ad pietatem, sed
naturaliter nobis inesse dicit; apostolicis dogmatibus
adversarius approbatur, beato Paulo dicente: *Confidimus*

* nobis, Gennad.

* So Gennad.,
but Hard. reads
generationem.

---

7 From Gennadius, ibid. § 41.   We may compare with this Article
S. Aug. cont. d. Ep. Pel. IV. (iv.) § 12, in which he shows that
the passage, *Si volueritis et audieritis me* (Is. i. vv. 19, 20), does not
imply that will precedes grace, which would be inconsistent with the
words, *Præparatur voluntas a Domino* (Prov. viii. 35), and destroy the
whole character of grace.   S. Augustine, however, does not generally
speak of preventing grace as the work of the Holy Spirit, whose
special work, according to his teaching, is to infuse the motive of
Christian love in the regenerate.

8 From Gennadius, ibid. § 42.   Cf. Aug. De Præd. Sanct. (ii.)
§§ 3, 4 : *Sed nunc eis respondendum esse video, qui divina testimonia,
quæ de hac re adhibuimus, ad hoc dicunt valere, ut noverimus ex
nobis quidem nos habere ipsam fidem, sed incrementum ejus ex Deo,*

IV. That God to cleanse us from sin does not wait for, but prepares our will.

If any one contends that God to cleanse us from sin waits for our will, and does not rather allow that our very wish to be cleansed is put into us by the infusion and operation of the Holy Spirit, he resists the Spirit Himself, who says by Solomon, "The will is prepared by the Lord," and the Apostle who teaches the wholesome doctrine, "It is God who worketh in you both to will and to perform for His good will."

V. That the beginning of faith is not of ourselves, but of the grace of God.

If any one says that just as the increase, so also the beginning of faith, and the very feeling of belief by which we believe on Him who justifies the "impious" man, and come to the Regeneration of sacred Baptism, is not by the gift of grace (*i.e.*, by the inspiration of the Holy Spirit correcting our will from infidelity to faith, from impiety to piety), but is implanted in us by nature, he is proved an adversary to the doctrines of the Apostle; for the blessed Paul says, "We trust that He who began a

---

tanquam fides non ab ipso donetur nobis, sed ab ipso tantum augeatur in nobis, eo merito quo cœpit a nobis. He then proceeds to argue from Rom. xi. 35 ; Phil. i. 29 ; 1 Cor. vii. 25 ; and from the conversion of S. Paul, that the beginning of faith must come from God. See also Cont. d. Ep. Pel. II. (x.) § 23, where he proves the same from Ps. lxxvi. (lxxvii.) 10, 11 : *Numquid obliviscetur misereri Deus? aut continebit in ira sua misericordias suas? Et dixi: nunc cœpi ; hæc mutatio dexteræ Excelsi.* He argues from this passage that the beginning of faith referred to in *nunc cœpi* must follow the mercy of God alluded to in ver. 10.

9 This, derived from Rom. iv. 5, became the technical word in theological language for an unregenerate man.

*quia qui cœpit in vobis bonum opus, perficiet usque in diem
Domini nostri Jesu Christi ; et illud : Vobis datum est
pro Christo non solum ut in eum credatis, sed etiam ut pro
illo patiamini ; et : Gratia salvi facti estis per fidem, et
hoc non ex vobis ; Dei enim donum est.* Qui enim fidem
qua in Deum credimus dicunt esse naturalem, omnes eos
qui ab Ecclesia Christi alieni sunt quodammodo fideles
esse definiunt.

VI. Quod sine gratia Dei credentibus et petentibus
misericordia non conferatur, cum gratia ipsa faciat
ut credamus et petamus.

Some MSS.
read orantibus.

¹⁰ Si quis sine gratia Dei credentibus, volentibus, deside-
rantibus, conantibus, laborantibus,* vigilantibus, studentibus, petentibus, quærentibus, pulsantibus nobis misericordiam dicit conferri divinitus, non autem ut credamus,
velimus, vel hæc omnia sicut opportet agere valeamus,

---

¹⁰ From Gennadius, ibid. § 43. This Article sums up and expands
the last three. It may be divided into four heads. Preventing
grace is not in any case preceded (1) by faith (*credentibus*); (2) by
will (*volentibus, desiderantibus*) ; (3) by human effort (*conantibus—
studentibus*) ; (4) by prayer (*petentibus—pulsantibus*). To these we
may add obedience and humility, which is closely connected with, if
not implied in, 3 and 4. Of these the first has been already treated of
in Art. V. It is constantly insisted on by S. Augustine as, *e.g.*, in De
Præd. Sanct. (vii.) § 12, where he shows that faith is not a work in
the ordinary sense, but the work of God. The second is the subject
of Art. IV. It is quoted by Prosper as being the opinion of Cassian
(See Anti-Pelag. Treat. Introd. pp. lx. lxi.), in Cont. Coll. (iv.)
§§ 11, 12 ; (xix.) § 55 and passim. Cf. also Aug. De Spir. et Lit.

good work in you will perfect it even unto the day of our Lord Jesus Christ;" and also, "To you it was given in behalf of Christ, not only to believe in Him, but also to suffer for Him;" and again, "By grace ye were saved by faith, and that not out of yourselves, for it is the gift of God." For those who say that the faith by which we believe in God is by nature, define all those who do not belong to the Church of Christ as in a certain sense "faithful."

VI. That without the grace of God mercy is not bestowed upon us when we believe and seek for it; rather it is grace itself which causes us to believe and seek for it.

If any one says that without the grace of God mercy is bestowed upon us by God when we believe, wish, long for it, strive, toil, watch, desire it, seek, ask for it, or when we knock, and does not rather acknowledge that it is by the infusion and inspiration of the Holy Spirit within us that we believe, wish, or have the power of

---

(xxxiv.).§ 60 : *profecto et ipsum velle credere Deus operatur in homine.* The third is a condemnation of the Pelagian doctrine in its extreme form. The fourth is a repetition in sense, though not in form, of the error condemned in Art. III. Cassian and others who held Pelagian or semi-Pelagian views were constantly appealing to our Lord's words, "Ask, and it shall be given unto you, seek, and ye shall find, knock, and it shall be opened unto you" (Matt. vii. 7), in favour of their view that prayer and effort must precede grace. Prosper quotes and refutes this argument of Cassian in Cont. Coll. (ii.) § 6. Cf. also S. Aug. De Don. Pers. (xxiii.) § 64 : *Attendant ergo quomodo falluntur qui putant esse a nobis, non dari nobis, ut petamus, quæramus, pulsemus,* and so on.

per infusionem et inspirationem Sancti Spiritus in nobis
fieri confitetur, et aut humilitati aut obedientiæ humanæ
subjungit gratiæ adjutorium, nec ut obedientes et humiles
simus, ipsius gratiæ donum esse consentit; resistit apostolo dicenti : *Quid habes quod non accepisti?* et : *Gratia
Dei sum id quod sum.*

VII. Quod viribus naturæ bonum aliquid quod ad salutem pertineat, cogitare aut eligere sine gratia non
possimus.

[11] Si quis per naturæ vigorem bonum aliquid, quod ad
salutem pertinet vitæ æternæ, cogitare ut expedit aut
eligere, sive salutari, id est evangelicæ prædicationi consentire posse confirmat absque illuminatione et inspiratione
Spiritus Sancti, qui dat omnibus suavitatem in consen-
tiendo et credendo veritati : hæretico fallitur Spiritu, non
intelligens vocem Dei in Evangelio dicentis : *Sine me
nihil potestis facere*, et illud Apostoli : *Non quod idonei
simus cogitare aliquid a nobis, quasi ex nobis, sed sufficientia
nostra ex Deo est.*

---

[11] From Gennadius, ibid. § 44. This Article describes the work
of the Spirit on the mind and heart. The first produces thought,
consent, and belief ; the second, pleasure and delight in believing.
For the first cf. Aug. De Don. Pers. (xiii.) § 33 : *Cogitantes credimus, cogitantes loquimur, cogitantes agimus quicquid agimus :
quod autem attinet ad pietatis viam et verum Dei cultum non sumus
idonei cogitare aliquid tanquam ex nobismet ipsis, sed sufficientia
nostra ex Deo est.* On the other hand, in De Spir. et Lit. (xxxiv.)
§ 60, S. Augustine speaks of consent to the call of God as an act
of the will. *Consentire autem vocationi Dei vel ab ea dissentire*

doing all these things as we ought, and puts the help of grace as a supplement to human humility or obedience, instead of acknowledging that obedience and humility are the gift of grace itself, he resists the Apostle who says, "What hast thou which thou hast not received?" and, "By the grace of God I am what I am."

VII. That by the powers of nature without grace we are not able to think or choose any good thing pertaining to our salvation.

If any one affirms that we can fitly think or choose any good thing pertaining to the salvation of eternal life, or agree to the saving, *i.e.*, the evangelical, preaching by the strength of nature without the illumination and inspiration of the Holy Spirit, who gives to all pleasure in agreeing and believing the truth, he is deceived by an heretical Spirit, not understanding the words of God, who says in the gospel, "Without me ye can do nothing;" and those again of the Apostle, "Not that we are fitted to think anything of ourselves as from ourselves, but our sufficiency is from God."

---

propriæ voluntatis est. In his early works S. Augustine clearly recognized in the act of choice two distinct elements, the human will and the work of the Spirit guiding it and assisting it in its choice, but not overruling it. Latterly, however, he seems to have underrated the first, and made Divine grace practically an overruling power. The action of the Spirit on the heart of man, inflaming it to love, is one of the leading themes of the *De Spiritu et Litera*. This is most beautifully expressed in (iii.) § 5, where he speaks of the soul as inflamed by the Spirit with a passionate longing to partake of the true Light. Cf. also (x.) § 16; (xxix.) § 51.

VIII. Quod per liberum arbitrium ad gratiam baptismi
pervenire nullus possit.

per misericor-
diam, Gennad.

¹² Si quis alios * misericordia, alios vero per liberum
arbitrium, quod in omnibus qui de prævaricatione primi
hominis nati sunt constat esse vitiatum, ad gratiam baptismi posse venire contendit; a recta fide probatur

ille, Gennad.

alienus.   * Is enim non omnium liberum arbitrium per
peccatum primi hominis asserit infirmatum; aut certe ita
læsum putat, ut tamen quidam valeant sine revelatione

ministerium,
Gennad.

Dei *mysterium salutis æternæ per semetipsos posse
conquirere.   Quodquam sit contrarium ipse Dominus
probat, qui non aliquos, sed neminem ad se posse venire
testatur nisi quem Pater attraxerit, sicut et Petro dicit:
Beatus es Simon Barjona, qui caro et sanguis non reve-
lavit tibi, sed Pater meus qui in cælis est; et apostolus;
Nemo potest dicere Dominum Jesum nisi in Spiritu
Sancto.

IX. De adjutorio Dei, per quod bona operamur.

recta, Prosper.

¹³ Divini est muneris, cum et *recte cogitamus, et pedes

---

¹² From Gennadius, ibid. § 45.   The doctrine here condemned
was a speculation of Cassian.   It was especially attacked by Prosper
in his *Contra Collatorem.*   See especially (iii.) § 9 : *alii sint quos*
gratia Dei salvet, alii quos lex et natura. (vii.) § 18 : *hoc posse*
quosdam per liberum arbitrum sine adjutorio Dei, and passim.   See
below, p. 49, note 38.

¹³ This article is taken from Prosper's Liber Sententiarum, xxii.   It
is remarkable as being one of those quotations (chiefly confined to
the first 35), which Prosper makes, not from S. Augustine's works,

VIII. That by free choice no one can come to the grace
of Baptism.

If any one while allowing that some receive that
benefit by God's mercy, contends that others however
can come to the grace of baptism by their free choice
(which in all who were born after the transgression of the
first man is known to have been impaired) is proved not
to belong to the true faith. For he asserts that the free
choice of all men was not weakened by the sin of the
first man ; or at least, thinks that it was only so far
injured as to admit of the possibility of some being able
to seek for themselves the mystery of eternal salvation
without the revelation of God. How false this opinion
is is proved by the Lord Himself, who testifies not that
some, but that *no one* can come to Him unless the Father
draw him ; just as he says also to Peter, " Blessed art
thou, Simon Barjona, because flesh and blood hath not
revealed it to thee, but My Father which is in heaven,"
and the Apostle, " No man can say the Lord Jesus, except
by the Holy Spirit."

IX. Of the help of God, by which we do good
works.

It is of God's gift when we think rightly, and keep our

but from his own. This particular quotation is taken from Prosper's
work on Psalm cxviii. (cxix.) v. 59 ; but it is in the strictest accordance with the teaching of S. Augustine. Cf. especially De Nat.
et Grat., (xxvii.) § 30, where the doctrine that all good works
come from God is based on Phil. ii. 12, 13, *Deus in homine et velle et
operari operatur;* and Serm. xiii., (iii.) 3 : *Si ergo Deus est qui
operatur in nobis, quare dictum est,* " *Vestram ipsorum salutem
operamini.*" *Quia sic in nobis operatur, ut et nos operemur.*

nostros a falsitate et injustitia continemus; quoties enim
bona agimus, Deus in nobis atque nobiscum ut operemur
operatur.

X. De adjutorio Dei ab omnibus semper implor-
ando.

* Some MSS.
read sanatis.

[14] Adjutorium Dei etiam renatis ac * sanctis semper est
implorandum, ut ad finem bonum pervenire, vel in bono
possint opere perdurare.

XI. De obligatione votorum.

* voveret, Prosp.
Aug.
* acciperet,
Prcsp. Aug.

[15] Nemo quidquam Domino recte *voverit, nisi ab ipso
* acceperit quod voveret, sicut legitur: *Quæ de manu tua
accepimus damus tibi.*

---

[14] This is the only article not derived almost verbally from some
other source. But the doctrine that perseverance is necessary as
well as Regeneration, and is only attainable by Divine grace, is laid
great stress on by S. Augustine, and made the subject of a special
treatise, called De Dono Perseverantiæ. In the beginning of this
work, (ii.) § 4—(v.) § 9, he grounds the duty of prayer for perseverance on St. Cyprian's interpretation of the several clauses in the
Lord's Prayer. In (vi.) § 10, he explains that by perseverance he
means *perseverantia usque in finem.* In (vii.) § 15, he escapes the
difficulty of reconciling prayer for perseverance with his view of
Predestination by the remark, *Prorsus in hac re non operosas dispu-
tationes exspectet ecclesia, sed attendat quotidianas orationes suas.*

steps from falsehood and unrighteousness ; for as often as we do good, God works in us and with us that we may work.

X. Of the help of God, how it is always to be implored by all.

The help of God is always to be implored even by those who are reborn and sanctified (healed), that they may be able to arrive at a good end, or endure in good works.

XI. Of the obligation of vows.

No one can properly vow anything to God, without having received what he would vow from Him, as it is read, "We give Thee what we have received from Thy hand."

---

[15] As far as *voveret* from Prosper, Lib. Sent. liv. He adapts it from S. Aug. De Civ. Dei, XVII. iv. 7 ; but neither he nor S. Augustine have the quotation from 1 Chron. xxix. 14, at the end. The doctrine here condemned is virtually that known in later times as that of works of supererogation, from which an *a fortiore* argument was drawn by the Pelagians in favour of human merit. The special works referred to in this argument were vows of chastity. See De Gest. Pel. (ch. xiii.) § 29. The article condemns the doctrine, not by denying works of supererogation, but by showing that even these are conditional upon Divine grace. Compare the rather different view taken in our Article XIV.

XII. Quales nos diligat Deus.

[16] Tales nos amat Deus quales futuri sumus ipsius dono, non quales sumus nostro [17] merito.

XIII. De reparatione liberi arbitrii.

[18] Arbitrium *voluntatis, in primo homine infirmatum, nisi per gratiam [19] baptismi non potest reparari; quod amissum, nisi a quo potuit dari, non potest reddi, unde

---

[16] From Prosper, Lib. Sent. lvi. It is not an actual quotation from S. Augustine, but may have been suggested by the following passage in the De Trinitate, IV. (i.) § 2 : *Ac primum nobis persuadendum fuit quantum nos diligeret Deus, ne disputatione non auderemus erigi in eum. Quales autem dilexerit, ostendi opportebat, ne tanquam de meritis nostris superbientes magis ab eo resiliremus, et in nostra fortitudine magis deficeremus.* See also De Cat. Rud. (iv.) § 7, where he argues the same from passages like Rom. v. 6 ; 1 John iii. 16 ; and adds, *Nulla est major ad amorem invitatio, quam prævenire amando.*

[17] The idea of human merit was not denied altogether by S. Augustine, but it was limited to works done after and by the grace of God. Grace itself could not be merited by man. See Art. XVIII. note. There is no question here of the nature of Predestination, whether it depends on Prescience or Absolute Purpose : the language of the Article is quite consistent with either view.

[18] From Gennad. Lib. de Eccles. Dogm. § 47, who adapted it from Prosper, Lib. Sent. clii. Except for the omission of the words *proprio vitio* after *amissum*, he has quoted it exactly from Augustine, De Civ. Dei, XIV. xi. 1. The passage runs thus : *Arbitrium igitur voluntatis tunc est vere liberum, cum vitiis peccatisque non servit. Tale datum est a Deo : quod amissum proprio vitio nisi a quo,* &c., as in text. S. Augustine did not mean that the natural power or faculty of choice itself was lost, but that by inherited depravity it had become enslaved to sin, and therefore its freedom was lost, until it was restored by God who gave it. In Cont. d. Ep. I. (iii.) § 6, he distinctly maintains that

XII. On what ground God loves us.

God loves us for what we shall be by His gift, not for what we are by our own merit.

XIII. Of the restoration of free choice.

The choice of the will, weakened in the first man, cannot be restored but by the grace of baptism; for being lost, it cannot be given back except by Him who

---

in a certain sense not merely *arbitrium voluntatis*, but *liberum arbitrium*, remained even after the fall, because the freedom was only hampered in one direction. It was free to commit sin, but not free to do good ; *Quæ potestas* (*i.e.*, the power of becoming sons of God), *nulla esse potest ex libero arbitrio, quia nec liberum in bono erit, quod liberator non liberaverit; sed in malo liberum habet arbitrium*, &c. In De Civ. Dei, XIV. xi. 7, he speaks of the will of Adam before the fall as a *bona voluntas. Fecit itaque Deus hominem rectum : ac per hoc voluntatis bonæ. Non enim rectus esset, bonam non habens voluntatem.* Somewhat similarly in Op. Imperf. VI. xxv. (vol. x. p. 1346 in Benedictine edition), he divides *arbitrium liberum* into two parts : (1) a love of doing good ; (2) a love of happiness. The first was lost at the fall, the second is immovably fixed in human nature, and can never be lost ; but in order to work for good it must be assisted by Divine grace. *Hoc est liberum arbitrium nostris mentibus immobiliter fixum, non quo bene agere volumus, nam id humana iniquitate potuimus amittere, et gratia divina possumus recipere: sed liberum arbitrium quo beati esse volumus, et miseri nolumus, nec miseri possunt amittere nec beati.* . . . *Hoc arbitrium liberum adjuvatur per Dei gratiam, ut quod naturaliter volumus, hoc est beate vivere, bene vivendo habere possimus.*

[19] The insertion of the special reference to baptism as the remedy for original sin is characteristic of the Council, and important when we consider how seldom it made any alterations in the extracts from Patristic writers. The doctrine, however, was definitely taught by S. Augustine, and is implied of course in the whole of his argument as to the fate of unbaptized children. See above Introd. p. 9.

veritas ipsa dicit: *Si vos filius liberaverit, tunc vere liberi eritis.*

XIV. Quod ut liberemur a miseria, misericordia Dei prævenimur.

[20] Nullus miser de quacumque miseria liberatur, nisi qui Dei misericordia prævenitur, sicut dicit Psalmista: *Cito ⃰ anticipet nos misericordia ⃰ tua, Domine;* et illud: *Deus meus, misericordia ejus præveniet me.*

⃰ So Prosper. Some MSS. have anticipent—misericordiæ.

XV. Quod per gratiam Dei in melius mutetur fidelis.

[21] Ab eo quod formavit Deus mutatus est Adam, sed in pejus per iniquitatem suam: ab eo quod operata est iniquitas ⃰ mutatur fidelis, sed in melius per gratiam Dei. Illa ergo mutatio fuit prævaricatoris primi, hæc ⃰ secundum ⃰ Psalmistam *mutatio est dexteræ Excelsi.*

⃰ mutantur fideles, Prosper. Aug.

⃰ Om. Prosper.

---

[20] Taken from Prosper, Lib. Sent. ccxi. (ccxii.), with the addition of the two quotations. Prosper adapted it probably from such passages of S. Augustine as Op. Imperf. I. xc. : *In paradiso enim diabolus seductor beatæ voluntatis fuit, quam seducendo miseram fecit: nunc autem, sicut fateris, seductor est miseræ voluntatis. Ab hac ergo miseria. . . . non eam liberat nisi ille ad quem quotidie tota clamat Ecclesia, Ne nos inferas in tentationem,* &c. Compare also Enarr. in Ps. lxxviii. (lxxix.) § 11 : *Ad hoc vult intelligi anticipare nos misericordias Dei, ut nostra paupertas, id est infirmitas, eo miserante adjuvetur ad ejus præcepta facienda, ne ad judicium ejus damnandi veniamus.*

[21] Taken with slight alterations from Prosper, Lib. Sent. ccxxv. (ccxxvii.) Prosper has adapted it from the following passage of

could give it. Wherefore the truth Himself says: "If the Son shall make you free, ye shall be free indeed."

XIV. That to be freed from misery we are prevented by the mercy of God.

No miserable man is freed from any misery whatever, except he also is prevented by the mercy of God, as the Psalmist says, "Let Thy mercy speedily go before us, O Lord;" and again, "As for my God, His mercy will prevent me."

XV. That through the grace of God a faithful man is changed for the better.

Adam was changed from that which God formed him, but for the worse through his iniquity; a faithful man is changed from that which sin has wrought, but for the better through the grace of God. The former therefore was the change of the first transgressor; the latter is "the change of the right hand of the Most High."

S. Augustine, Enarr. in Ps. lxviii.   Serm. i. § 2: *Ab eo quod forma-vit Deus, mutatus est Adam, sed in pejus iniquitatis suæ: ab eo quod operata est iniquitas, mutantur fideles, sed in melius per gratiam Dei. Ut mutaremur in pejus, nostra iniquitas fuit, ut mutaremur in melius, non nostra justititia, sed gratia Dei præstat.*   The substi-tution by Prosper of the words *mutatio est dexteræ Excelsi* from Ps. lxxvi. 11 (lxxvii. 10), for *gratia Dei* in the last clause, is in ac-cordance with S. Augustine's interpretation of the psalm in Cont. d. Ep. Pel. II. (x.) § 23. *Et dixi, nunc cæpi, hæc mutatio dexteræ excelsi.   Cum ergo dixisset nunc cæpi; non ait, hæc mutatio arbitrii mei, sed dexteræ excelsi.*   On the various translations and interpre-tations of this difficult verse see Delitzsch on the Psalms *in loco.* See also note on Art. V. above.

4

XVI. Quod ex eo quod habemus, non sit gloriandum, cum ex Deo sit.

[22] Nemo ex eo quod videtur habere glorietur, tanquam non acceperit, aut ideo se putet accepisse, quia litera extrinsecus vel ut legeretur apparuit, vel ut audiretur * sonuit. Nam † sicut Apostolus dicit †: *Si per legem iustitia, ergo Christus gratis mortuus est.* * *Ascendens in altum* † *captivavit captivitatem, dedit dona hominibus.* Inde habet quicunque habet : quisquis autem se inde habere negat, aut vere non habet, aut id quod * videtur habere † aufertur ab eo.

(margin notes:)
* insonuit, Prosp. Aug.
† Om. Prosp. Aug.
* See note.
ascendit, Aug.
† captivam duxit, Prosp Aug.
* habet, some MSS., Aug. and Prosp.
† auferetur, some MSS., Aug. and Prosp.

XVII. De fortitudine Christiana.

(margin:) 1 John ii. 15, 16.

[23] Fortitudinem Gentilium [24] mundana cupiditas, fortitudinem autem Christianorum Dei caritas facit, quæ diffusa est in cordibus nostris, non per voluntatis arbitrium, quod

---

[22] Slightly altered from Prosper, Sent. cclix.(cclxi.), which is almost an exact quotation from Augustine, De Spir. et Lit. (xxix.) § 50. The omission of the words *Porro autem si non gratis mortuus est* before *ascendens, &c.*, spoils the sense, and is probably accidental, being due to *homœoteleuton*. To refute the view of Pelagius, that grace consisted mainly of an outward revelation or law, was the chief object of this treatise of S. Augustine. He bases his arguments on 2 Cor. iii. 6, where he interprets *litera* of an external revelation of law distinguished in principle from the internal infusion of grace by the Spirit.

[23] From Prosper, Lib. Sent. ccxcv. (ccxcvii.) It is a quotation from S. Augustine, Op. Imperf. I. lxxxiii. It is an answer to the argument of Julian from the Pelagian side, that the fortitude or power of enduring pain shown by heathens and Christians alike proves that no man can be either compelled into

XVI. That we should not boast of what we have, because
it is of God.   ·

Let no one boast of that which he seems to have, as
though he had not received it, or think that he has
therefore received it, because a letter from without has
either appeared for him to read, or sounded for him to
hear. For, as the Apostle says, "If righteousness is by
the law, then Christ died in vain." "Ascending up on
high, he made captivity captive, He gave gifts to men."
From that source he has it, whoever has ought; and
whoever denies that he has it from that source, either
has it not truly, or that which he seems to have is taken
away from him.

XVII. Of Christian courage.

The courage of heathens is due to worldly desire; but
the courage of Christians to the love of God, which is
spread abroad in our hearts, not through the choice of the

---

sin or rescued from it against his will. Julian's words are, *Ne homo
vel in peccatum a quoquam impellatur, vel a peccato abstrahatur,
voluntate captiva ; quam non posse capi, si dedi ipsa noluerit, testatur
fortitudo, cujus lacerti in contemptu dolorum et per Gentiles et per
Christianos assidue claruerunt.*

The whole subject is fully discussed in Augustine, De Patientia,
see especially (chs. xvi., xvii.) §§ 13, 14, where he argues from
such passages as 1 Cor. xiii. 4, 7, *Caritas magnanima est, omnia
tolerat,* that the motive of Christian courage is love. The motive of
heathen courage is *cupiditas,* by which he seems to understand
mere natural selfishness. The special example given is that of
criminals who are willing to endure the most painful tortures to
avoid death, which would follow if they confessed their crimes.

[24] The reference in *mundana cupiditas* is to 1 S. John ii. 15, 16.

* Some MSS.
read *a.*

est * in nobis, sed per Spiritum Sanctum, qui datus est nobis.

XVIII. Nullis meritis gratiam præveniri.

* After gratiam
some MSS. add
Dei.

[25] Nullis meritis gratiam * prævenientibus, debetur merces bonis operibus, si fiant; sed gratia quæ non debetur præcedit ut fiant.

XIX. Neminem nisi Deo miserante salvari.

* cum igitur,
Aug.
† posset, Gennad.
* potest, Prosp.
Aug.
† recuperare
Prosp. Aug.
* quam, Prosp.

[26] Natura humana, etiamsi in illa integritate, in qua est condita, permaneret, nullo modo seipsam, Creatore suo non adjuvante, servaret: * unde cum sine Dei gratia salutem non † possit custodire quam accepit, quomodo sine Dei gratia * poterit † reparare * quod perdidit?

---

[25] From *debetur merces* to the end is from Prosper, Sent. ccxcvii. (ccxcix.) Prosper adapted it from Aug. Op. Imperf. I. cxxxiii. *Debetur, inquam, bona merces operibus hominum bonis; sed non debetur gratia, quæ ipsos homines bonos operatur ex malis.*

The insertion of the first clause from the title of the sentence in Prosper, '*nullis meritis præveniri gratiam,*' is, as it happens, unfortunate, because it causes an ambiguity. The negative should not be carried on to the second clause. The meaning of S. Augustine is that a reward is owed for good works, because they are the works of God (see second quotation below), but no good works can merit grace. The proper order is grace, good works, reward, and this order cannot be reversed. The first clause rightly understood is exactly Augustinian. In the context of the passage just quoted, a few lines further down, he adds, *Istam gratiam vere gratiam, i.e., gratuitam nullisque meritis præcedentibus debitam, commendabat Apostolus.* In the next chapter he explains in what sense good works can, and in what they cannot, be said to have a meritorious value. *Lege Ezechielem prophetam unde quod satis visum est supra commemoravi:*

will which is in us, but by the Holy Spirit which has been
given us.

XVIII. That grace in not prevented by any merits.

A reward is not owed for any merits preventing grace
on the ground of good works done, but grace which is
not owed precedes to enable them to be done.

XIX. That no man is saved except by the mercy of
    God.

Human nature, even though it remained in that integrity
in which it was made, could in no way preserve itself
without the help of its Creator. Since then without the
grace of God it cannot keep the salvation which it has
received, how without the grace of God will it have the
power of restoring what it has lost?

---

*ista etiam verba reperies, i.e., Deum facere ut præcepta ejus homines
faciant, quorum miseretur, non propter merita eorum, quæ mala ibi
esse commemorat, sed propter nomen suum, ut Deo sine meritis eorum
faciente ut faciant præcepta ejus, incipiant merita bonorum habere
factorum. Hæc est gratia quam negatis, non ex operibas quæ fiunt,
sed ut fiant.* Comp. also Ep. cxciv. v. 19.

[26] From Gennadius, § 47, who quotes it from Prosper, Sent. cccviii.
(cccx.) with the single alteration of *recuperare quam* into *reparare
quod.* Prosper had already quoted it from S. Augustine, Ep. clxxxvi.
37. The necessity of grace, even in the unfallen state of Adam, is
more fully discussed in the Enchir. d. Fid. (civ.) § 28: *Quia etsi
peccatum in solo libero arbitrio erat constitutum, non tamen justitiæ
retinendæ sufficiebat liberum arbitrium, nisi participatione immutabilis
boni divinum adjutorium præberetur.* He goes on to compare
the state of the body, which may kill itself by starvation by a mere
act of choice, but cannot keep itself alive without food. Comp.
De Nat. et Grat. xlviii. § 56.

XX. Nihil boni hominem posse sine Deo.

[27] Multa Deus facit in homine bona quæ non facit homo, nulla vero facit homo * bona quæ non Deus † præstat ut faciat homo.

XXI. De natura et gratia.

[28] Sicut eis qui volentes in lege justificari * [et] a gratia exciderunt verissime dicit Apostolus : *Si * in lege justitia est, ergo Christus gratis mortuus est;* sic * eis qui gratiam, quam commendat et percipit fides Christi, putant esse naturam, verissime dicitur : " Si † per naturam justitia est, ergo Christus gratis mortuus est." Jam hic enim erat lex, et non justificabat : jam hic erat et natura, et non justificabat. Ideo Christus non gratis mortuus est, ut et lex per illum impleretur qui dixit : *Non veni legem solvere, sed * adimplere;* et natura, per Adam perdita, per illum repararetur, qui dixit *venisse se quærere et salvare quod perierat.*

---

[27] From Prosper, Sent. cccxii. (cccxiv.), who quotes it from Aug. Cont. d. Ep. Pel. II. (ix.) § 21. S. Augustine had been explaining Prov. xvi. 1. *Hominis est præparare cor, et a Domino responsio linguæ.* The ' preparation of the heart,' he argued, must be understood of man using God's help, ' the answer of the tongue' of the work of God alone in man in answer to prayer. *Ideo quippe scriptum est, hominis est præparare cor, et a Domino responsio linguæ: quia homo præparat cor, non tamen sine adjutorio Dei, qui sic tangit cor, ut homo præparet cor. In responsione autem linguæ, id est, in eo quod præparato cordi lingua divina respondet, nihil operis habet homo, sed totum est a Domino Deo.* Ibid. (ix.) §§ 19, 20. Rather differently he speaks, in De Grat. and Lib. (xvii.) § 33, of the work of God

XX. How man can do no good thing without God.

God does many good things in man which man does not do ; but man does no good things which God does not give him the power of doing.

XXI. Of nature and grace.

Just as the Apostle says most truly to those who, wishing to be justified in the law, have fallen from grace, " If justice is in the law, then Christ died in vain ; " so to those who think that nature is the grace which is commended and received by faith in Christ, it is most truly said, " If justice is by nature, then Christ died in vain." For in the first case there was law and it did not justify, in the second there was nature as well, and it did not justify. Therefore Christ did not die in vain, in order that both the law might be fulfilled by Him, who said, " I came not to destroy the law, but to fulfil " ; and nature, destroyed through Adam, might be restored by Him who said that He " came to seek and to save what was lost."

---

only as being the first action of preventing grace, as distinguished from its subsequent co-operating action. *Ut ergo velimus sine nobis operatur, cum autem volumus, et sic volumus ut faciamus, nobiscum cooperatur, tamen sine illo vel operante ut velimus, vel cooperante cum volumus, ad bona pietatis opera nihil valemus.* Comp. our English Art. X.

[28] From Gennadius, Ibid. § 48, who quotes from Prosper, Lib. Sent. cccxv. (cccxvii.), and he again from S. Augustine, De Grat. et Lib. (xiii.) § 25. The differences are merely verbal. That grace cannot be defined as nature, which has no justifying power, as the Pelagians held, is refuted constantly by S. Augustine. See, *e.g.,* De Nat. et Grat. (xxxiv.) § 39 ; and above, Introd. p. 8, note 3.

XXII. De his quæ hominum propria sunt.

²⁹ Nemo habet de suo nisi mendacium et peccatum ;
si quid autem habet homo veritatis atque justitiæ, ab illo
fonte est, quem debemus sitire in hac eremo, ut ex
eo quasi guttis quibusdam irrorati, non deficiamus
in via.

XXIII. De voluntate Dei et hominis.

³⁰ Suam voluntatem homines faciunt, non Dei, quando
id agunt quod Deo displicet ; quando autem * id faciunt †
ut divinæ serviant voluntati, quamvis volentes agant, *
illius tamen voluntas est a quo et præparatur et jubetur
quod volunt.

* ita, Prosper.
† Some MSS. add
quod volunt from
Prosp. Aug.
* After *agant*
some MSS. read
quod agunt.

---

²⁹ From Prosper, Lib. Sent. cccxxiii. (cccxxv.), who quotes from
S. Aug. Tract. in Johan. v. 1. The last clause in S. Augustine runs
thus : *ut ne deficiamus in via, venire ad ejus requiem satietatemque
possimus.* This is his comment on S. John viii. 44.

³⁰ From Prosper, Lib. Sent. cccxxxviii. (cccxl.), who adopts it
from S. Aug. Tract. in Johan xix. § 19. S. Augustine, commenting
on the words in S. John v. 30, " I seek not my own will, but the
will of Him who sent me," writes : *Non meam, non propriam ; non
meam . . . quæ resistat Deo, Faciunt enim homines voluntatem suam,
non Dei, quando faciunt quod volunt, non quod jubet Deus : quando
autem ita faciunt quod volunt, ut tamen sequantur voluntatem Dei,
non faciunt voluntatem suam, quamvis quod volunt faciant. Volens fac
tuam quod juberis ; atque ita et hoc facies quod vis, et non voluntatem
facies sed jubentis.* What S. Augustine wishes to emphasize is that

XXII. Of the things which properly belong to men.

No man has anything of his own but falsehood and sin ; but if any man has any truth and justice, he has it from that fountain which we ought to thirst for in this desert, that being refreshed by it as with drops of water we may not faint by the way.

XXIII. Of the will of God and man.

Men do their own will, not that of God, when they do that which is displeasing to God ; but when they do (that which they will) in such a way as to serve the Divine will, although they act willingly, it is really the will of Him by whom their will is prepared and ordered.

---

the test of the action is the motive. If the first and leading motive of a man's action is the carrying out of his own will, it is wrong, rather on the ground that he is doing his own will, than that the action is from other grounds displeasing to God. The first motive should be to do God's will. But this does not necessarily imply that it is contrary to man's own will. On the contrary, it is his positive duty so to yield himself to God's will as to make it his own. The whole passage implies a real effort on the human side. This is not so distinctly brought out in the article itself, though it is perhaps more in accordance with the usual language of S. Augustine. The paradox in the clause *quando—voluntati* is much like our translation of *cui servire regnare est* (in the old Gelasian prayer) ' whose service is perfect freedom."

XXIV. De palmitibus vitis.

[31] Ita sunt in vite palmites, ut viti *nihil conferant, sed inde accipiant unde vivant : † sic quippe † vitis est in palmitibus, ut vitale alimentum subministret eis, non sumat ab eis. Ac per hoc et manentem in se habere Christum, et manere in Christo, discipulis prodest * utrumque, non Christo. Nam, præciso palmite, potest de viva radice alius pullulare ; qui autem præcisus est, sine radice non potest vivere.

XXV. De dilectione qua diligimus Deum.

[32] Prorsus donum Dei est diligere Deum. Ipse ut diligeretur dedit, qui non dilectus* diligit. Displicentes amati sumus, ut fieret in nobis unde placeremus. † Diffundit enim caritatem in cordibus nostris Spiritus Patris et Filii, quem cum Patre amamus et Filio.

Margin notes:

* Non, Aug.

† ita vero, Aug.

* So Prosp. Aug.; but the MSS. read *utcumque* (see note).

* dilexit, Prosp.

† diffudit, Prosp.

---

[31] With the exception of *utrumque* for *utcumque*, which is probably simply an accidental error in the MSS., this Art. is taken without alteration from Prosper, Sent. ccclxvi. (ccclxviii.) It is quoted, with slight alterations, from S. Aug. Tract. in Johan. lxxxi. § 1, where S. Augustine argues against the Pelagian theory of good works having a meritorious value on their own account. The metaphor of the vine always has been a favourite one in connection with this subject, because it shows that the grace of Christ is a real energizing power in man, not merely the forgiveness of sins. Compare, for example, the Decrees of the Council of Trent, Sess. VI. cap. xvi. ‘*Cum enim ille ipse Christus Jesus, tamquam caput in membra, et tamquam vitis in palmites, in ipsos justificatos jugiter virtutem influat : quæ virtus bona eorum opera semper antecedit et comitatur et subsequitur, et sine qua nullo pacto Deo grata,*

XXIV. Of the branches of the vine.

The branches are in the vine in such a way that
they bestow nothing on the vine, but from it receive the
power of life ; in such a way is the vine in the branches,
that it supplies them with the nourishment. of life, but
does not receive it from them. In the same way to
have Christ abiding in them and to abide in Christ were
both of advantage to the disciples, not to Christ. For if
a branch be cut off, another may spring up from the
living root ; but the branch which is cut off cannot live
without a root.

XXV. Of the love by which we love God.

To love God is entirely God's gift. He Himself has
given us the power of loving Him, who loves us, even
when we have not yet loved Him. When we were displeasing Him we were loved, that the power of pleasing
Him might be wrought in us, for charity is spread abroad
in our hearts by the Spirit of the Father and the Son,
whom with the Father and the Son we love.

---

et meritoria esse possent: and our own English Arts. X.–XIV.
which, while they deny the meritorious value of works altogether,
yet agree in attributing good works to the operation of God's grace,
and regarding them as the necessary consequences of a lively faith,
and as therefore pleasing to God.

[32] From Prosper, Liber Sent. ccclxx. (ccclxxii.) curtailed from
S. Augustine, Tract. in Johan. cii, § 5. S. Augustine argues that
S. John xvi. 27, " For the Father Himself loveth you, because ye
have loved Me," must be explained by 1 John iv. 10, " Herein is
love, not that we loved God, but that He loved us." So that the
disciples' love for Christ was first infused by God. On the love of
God being the great work of the Holy Spirit, compare the De
Spir. et Lit. (iii.) § 5, and passim.

³³ * Ac sic secundum suprascriptas sanctarum Scripturarum sententias vel antiquorum patrum definitiones, hoc Deo propitiante et praedicare debemus et credere, quod per peccatum primi hominis * inclinatum et attenuatum † fuerit liberum arbitrium, ut nullus postea aut diligere Deum sicut oportuit, aut credere in Deum, aut operari propter Deum quod bonum est possit, nisi eum gratia misericordiae divinae praevenerit. ³⁴ Unde et Abel justo, et Noe, et Abrahae, et Isaac, et Jacob, et omni antiquorum patrum multitudini, illam praeclaram fidem, quam in ipsorum laude praedicat Apostolus Paulus, non per bonum naturae quod prius in Adam datum † est, sed per gratiam Dei credimus fuisse collatam.   Quam gratiam etiam post adventum Domini omnibus ³⁵ qui baptizari desiderant, non in libero arbitrio haberi, sed Christi novimus simul et credimus largitate conferri, secundum illud quod saepe jam dictum est, et quod praedicat Paulus Apostolus: *Vobis donatum est pro Christo non solum ut in eum credatis, sed etiam ut pro illo patiamini;* et illud : *Deus qui coepit in vobis bonum opus, perficiet usque in diem Domini nostri Jesu Christi;* et illud : *Gratia salvi facti estis per fidem, et hoc non ex vobis, Dei donum est ;* et quod de se ipso ait Apostolus : *Misericordiam consecutus sum ut fidelis essem ;* non dixit "quia eram" sed "*ut essem ;*" et illud : *Quid habes quod non accepisti?* et illud : *Omne datum bonum et omne donum perfectum desursum est, descendens a Patre luminum ;* et illud : *Nemo habet quidquam,* * *nisi illi datum fuerit*

Marginal notes:

* Om. *ac sic* Gennad.

* *ita* before *incl.,* Gennad.
† *sit*, Gennad.

† Some MSS. read fuerat.

* Some MSS. add boni.

³³ This summary of the subject contained in the following paragraphs is taken almost verbatim from Gennadius, Lib. de Eccles. Dogm. §§ 49–51.

³⁴ On the patriarch's need of grace, cf. De Nat. et Grat. (xxxviii.) § 45 ; De Civ. Dei, xv. 1, 2 ; De Perf. Just. (xix.) § 42.

And so, in accordance with the above-mentioned opinions from the holy Scriptures, or the definitions of the ancient fathers, we ought by God's mercy both to teach and believe this, that through the sin of the first man free choice was so biassed and weakened that no one can afterwards either love God as he ought, or believe in God, or work for God's sake what is good, unless the grace of Divine mercy prevents him. Wherefore just Abel and Noe and Abraham and Isaac and Jacob, and the whole multitude of old fathers, we believe, had not that glorious faith which the Apostle Paul praises through natural goodness which was first implanted in Adam, but that it was bestowed upon them by the grace of God. This grace, even after the advent of our Lord, we know and believe that all who desire to be baptized have, not as dependent on free choice, but that it is bestowed upon them by the bounty of Christ, according to what has often been already mentioned, and what the Apostle Paul teaches, "To you it has been given for Christ, not only to believe on Him, but also to suffer for Him ; " and again, " God who has begun in you a good work, will perfect it until the day of our Lord Jesus Christ ; " and again, " By grace were ye made whole by faith, and that not of yourselves, it is the gift of God ; " and what the Apostle says of himself, "I obtained mercy, that I might be faithful ; " he did not say, "because I was," but "that I might be ; " and again, "What hast thou

---

35 The words *qui baptizari desiderant* must be explained consistently with Art. VI. and the concluding paragraph of this summary ; both of which are quoted from the same writer. In all who as a fact desire baptism, the desire itself is the result, not the condition of God's grace. See also Arts. V., VIII.

desuper. Innumerabilia sunt sanctarum Scripturarum testimonia, quæ possunt ad probandam gratiam proferri, sed brevitatis studio prætermissa sunt, quia et revera cui pauca non sufficiunt, plura non proderunt.

36 Hoc etiam secundum fidem Catholicam credimus, quod accepta per baptismum gratia, omnes baptizati, Christo auxiliante et cooperante, quæ ad salutem animæ pertinent possint et debeant, si fideliter laborare voluerint, adimplere. 37 Aliquos vero ad malum divina potestate prædestinatos esse, non solum non credimus, sed etiam si sunt qui tantum malum credere velint, cum omni detestatione illis anathema dicimus.

* Hoc etiam salubriter profitemur et credimus, quod in omni opere bono non nos incipimus, et postea per Dei misericordiam adjuvamur, sed ipse nobis, nullis præce-

* Om. Hoc—credimus Gennad.

---

36 This lays stress on the importance, in case of those who have received grace in baptism, of combining their own effort with the co-operating grace of God. This effort cannot, in the first instance, lay claim on God's grace (see Art. VI.), but afterwards is necessary to work out salvation.

37 This is remarkable as being the only statement in which the Council or Gennadius, whom it quotes, differs considerably from the teaching of S. Augustine. It cannot be seriously doubted that what is here condemned is what is usually known as the doctrine of Reprobation, viz., that certain persons were decreed from eternity to be lost. The word *malum* was probably used by Gennadius advisedly. It introduced the great moral objection to the doctrine that it imputes *evil* to God. This objection had been already answered to his own satisfaction by S. Augustine (Cont. d. Ep. Pel. II. (vii.) § 13.) by explaining that it was only evil as looked at from man's view, not from God's : *Ei cui redditur malum est, quia supplicium ejus est, ei vero a quo redditur bonum est, quia recte factum ejus est.* (This passage is referred to by Dr. Bright, Anti - Pel. Treat. Intr. p. lxvi., note 2.) It is true that S. Augustine usually treats this side of the doctrine of Predestination negatively. He

which thou hast not received ? " and again, " Every good gift and every perfect gift is from above, coming down from the Father of lights ; " and again, " No one has anything unless it has been given him from above." There are numberless passages of Scripture which may be brought forward to prove grace, but for the sake of brevity we have omitted to mention them, because he who is not satisfied with few will certainly not be convinced by more.

This too we believe, according to the Catholic faith, that when grace has been received by baptism, all baptized persons, by the help and co-operation of Christ, may and ought, if they wish to labour faithfully, accomplish all things which pertain to the salvation of the soul. But that any are by the Divine power predestined to evil, we not only do not believe, but if there are any who would believe such an evil doctrine, we altogether detest them and anathematize them.

---

preferred to dwell on the bright side, so to speak, of God's purposes. The word " predestined " is almost exclusively used of those predestined to eternal life ; but there are quite enough passages to show, however much we might wish to the contrary, that S. Augustine, in his later life at any rate, did believe that the wicked were positively, not merely negatively or even contingently, included in the eternal decrees of God. Such expressions as *prædestinati in interitum* can hardly be otherwise understood. See for example Tract. in Johan. xlviii. §§ 4–6 : *Quomodo ergo istis dixit, " Non estis ex ovibus meis ? Quia videbat eos ad sempiternum interitum prædestinatos, non ad vitam æternam sui sanguinis pretio comparatos. . . . Quid potest fur et latro."* *Non perdunt nisi ad interitum prædestinatos.* He argues in De An. et Or. IV. (x.) § 16, that the punishment of such is just on the ground of original sin. *Qui (Deus) est et illis quos prædestinavit ad æternam mortem justissimus supplicii retributor : non solum propter illa, quæ volenti adjiciunt, verum etiam si infantes nihil adjiciant, propter originale peccatum.* See also De Perf. Just. (xiii.) § 31.

dentibus bonis meritis, et fidem et amorem sui prius
inspirat, ut et [38] baptismi sacramenta fideliter requiramus,
et post baptismum cum ipsius adjutorio ea quæ sibi sunt
placita implere possimus. Unde manifestissime creden-
dum est, quod et illius latronis quem Dominus ad paradisi
patriam revocavit, [39] et Cornelii centurionis ad quem an-

---

[38] The language and conceptions of theology are, so to speak, based
on the theory of Adult Baptism. Faith and love and personal effort,
none of which can exist actually in an infant, are here spoken of as
naturally, if not necessarily, preceding baptism itself. Similarly our
Church Catechism speaks of faith and repentance as the necessary
conditions of baptism. The Council of Trent, following Thomas.
Aquinas, escaped the difficulty by practically limiting the doctrine of
preventing grace to those who are baptized as adults, and must first
receive both the inward and outward preparation necessary. The
doctrine that an infant, though he cannot have actual faith, may
have a *habitus fidei*, does not explain this difficulty, because, according to the language of the schoolmen, the *habitus fidei* was
conferred by baptism, ard did not precede it.

S. Augustine explained the difficulty of connecting the doctrine of
preventing grace and its working with Infant Baptism, by saying
that the faith and will of the parents in those who offered the
child, availed for it. This he said was by the power of the One
Spirit : *Regenerans ergo Spiritus in majoribus offerentibus et parvulo
oblato renatoque communis est : ideo per hanc societatem unius ejusdem
que spiritus prodest offerentium voluntas parvulo oblato.* Ep. xcviii.—
(xxiii.) § 2. Lower down, § 9, he argues that faith and conversion
only belong to the child sacramentally in baptism, that is to say,
they are symbolised, but are not yet actually realised. He then
proceeds to show (§ 10) that as the child grows up and becomes
endued with reason, his own will must actually accord with the
truth of the sacrament. *Cum autem homo sapere cœperit, non
illud sacramentum repetet, sed intelliget, ejusque veritati consonâ
etiam voluntate coaptabitur.* If a man refuse to believe, he is the real
infidel, not the baptized child, who, though he cannot believe in
thought, yet does not resist the faith, and will be saved through
the prayers of the Church by Christ's help. S. Augustine wrote
rather differently in his treatise De Bapt. c. Don. III. (xiv.) § 19,

We also profess and believe this wholesome doctrine, that in every good work it is not ourselves who begin and are afterwards helped by the mercy of God, but God Himself first, without any precedent good merits, inspires us with His faith and love, that we may faithfully seek the sacred ordinances of baptism, and after baptism may by His help accomplish those things which are pleasing

where he argues that the faith of the receiver does not affect the efficacy of the sacrament. He implies, in fact, that faith before baptism must be imperfect, because men are still carnal, and he makes this the ground for not re-baptizing heretics or unbelievers.

With the earlier quotations from S. Augustine we may compare the answer to the difficulty in our Church Catechism, which lays the chief stress on the faith and repentance being realised in the after-life of the recipient, whereas at baptism they are only promised for him by his sureties. But that the English Church does not regard the efficacy of baptism itself, apart from its practical benefits, as dependent on faith and repentance, is clear from the Office for Private Baptism, wherein faith and repentance are not promised for the child.

[39] These were, according to the Pelagian idea, typical examples of men who had received mercy and pardon without preventing grace. Zacchæus and the robber were expressly instanced by Cassian in his fifth definition quoted by Prosper, Cont. Coll. vii. 17 : *Sin vero gratia Dei semper inspirari bonæ voluntatis principia dixerimus: quid de Zacchæi fide? quid de illius in cruce latronis pietate dicemus? qui desiderio suo vim quemdam regnis cælestibus inferentes* (alluding to Matt. xi. 12) *specialia vocationis monita prævenerunt*, and were so distinguished, he maintained, from S. Matthew and S. Paul, who were called by grace. So Prosper, Ad. Ruf. Ep. vi., refers in a similar way to the example of Cornelius. He concludes by saying, *Quo satis aperte ostenditur, omnia opera quæ in Cornelio præcesserunt, Dei gratiam ad emundationem ipsius inchoasse*. S. Augustine had himself discussed the subject still more fully in the De Præd. Sanct. (vii.) §12. He argued that the prayers and alms of Cornelius were the result in a certain measure of faith, which was itself the gift of God, as being the foundation of God's building, as distinguished from works, the superstructure.

* Some MSS.
read largitalis
donum.

gelus Domini missus est, et Zacchæi qui ipsum Dominum suscipere meruit, illa tam admirabilis fides non fuit de natura, sed divinæ * gratiæ largitate donata.

40 Et quia definitionem antiquorum patrum nostramque, quæ suprascripta est, non solum religiosis, sed etiam laicis medicamentum esse et desideramus et cupinus, placuit ut eam et illustres ac magnifici viri, qui nobiscum ad præfatam festivitatem convenerunt, propria manu subscriberent.

SUBSCRIPTIONES EPISCOPORUM & ILLUSTRIUM VIRORUM.

Cæsarius in Christi nomine episcopus constitutionem nostram relegi, et subscripsi not. quinto nonas Julias, Deciore Juniore, viro clarissimo consule.

Julianus, amartolus episcopus, relegi et subscripsi.
Constantius in Christi nomine episcopus consensi et subscripsi.

Cyprianus	,,	,,	,,	,,
Eucherius	,,	,,	,,	,,
Item Eucherius	,,	,,	,,	,,
Heraclius	,,	,,	,,	,,
Principius	,,	,,	,,	,,

---

40 The doctrine of grace is one that connects itself morely closely and directly with our action and bearing towards God. As such it affects all laymen as well as the teachers of Christian doctrine. On this account the Council adopted the unusual custom of allowing

to Him. From this it most clearly follows that we should believe that the very praiseworthy faith of the robber whom the Lord recalled to the home of Paradise, and of Cornelius, the centurion, to whom the angel of the Lord was sent, and of Zacchæus, who was permitted to entertain our Lord Himself, was not of nature, but was given by the bounty of Divine grace.

And because we desire and wish the definition of the early fathers and of ourselves, above given, to be a healing not only to clergy but also to laity, we have thought good that the illustrious and noble men who have come together with us to the before-mentioned feast, should subscribe to it with their own hand.

SUBSCRIPTIONS OF THE BISHOPS AND ILLUSTRIOUS MEN.

I, Cæsarius, bishop in the name of Christ, have read over and subscribed our determination. Witness our hand on the 3rd of July, in the consulship of the most illustrious Decius,

I, Julianus, a sinful bishop, have read over and subscribed.

I, Constantius, bishop in the name of Christ, have consented and subscribed.

I, Cyprianus	,,	,,	,,	,,
I, Eucherius	,,	,,	,,	,,
I, also Eucherius	,,	,,	,,	,,
I, Heraclius	,,	,,	,,	,,
I, Principius	,,	,,	,,	,,

certain rich and influential laymen to sign its decrees. There seems to have been a slight difference in the form of signature adopted by some of the laity to that of the bishops, but the MSS. vary, and it is hardly safe, if otherwise satisfactory, to base any argument upon it.

Philagrius in Christi nomine episcopus consensi et subscripsi.

Maximus	,,	,,	,,	,,
Prætextatus	,,	,,	,,	,,
Alethius	,,	,,	,,	,,
Lupercianus	,,	,,	,,	,,
Vindemialis	,,	,,	,,	,,

PETRUS MARCELLINUS FELIX LIBERIUS, vir clarissimus et illustris Præfectus Prætorii Galliarum, atque patricius, consentiens subscripsi.

Syagrius, vir illustris consensi et subscripsi.

Opilio	,,	,,	,,
Pantagathus	,,	,,	,,

Deodatus, vir illustris consentiens subscripsi.

Carriatto	,,	,,	,,
Marcellus	,,	,,	,,

Namatius, vir illustris consensi et subscripsi.

I, Philagrius, bishop in the name of Christ, have consented and subscribed.

I, Maximus   „   „   „   „
I, Prætextatus   „   „   „   „
I, Alethius   ,,   „   „   „
I, Lupercianus   „   „   „   „
I, Vindemialis   ,,   „   „   „

I, Peter Marcellinus Felix Liberius, a most illustrious man and distinguished Prætorian-Prefect of Gaul, and Patrician, consent and have subscribed.

I, Syagrius, an illustrious man, have consented and subscribed.

I, Opilius   „   „   „   „
I, Pantagathius   „   „   „   „

I, Deodatus, an illustrious man, consent and have subscribed.

I, Carriatto   „   „   „   „
I, Marcellus   „   „   „   „

I, Namatius, an illustrious man, have consented and subscribed.

JAMES THORNTON'S

$\mathfrak{List\ of\ Publications}$

CHIEFLY EDUCATIONAL,

MANY IN USE AT THE HIGHER SCHOOLS AND UNIVERSITIES.

CONTENTS.

Also Sold by SIMPKIN, MARSHALL, & CO., London.

A Catalogue of these Publications with fuller descriptions, some notices from the press, and specimen pages, will be issued shortly, and will be forwarded gratis on application.

JAMES THORNTON *desires to direct attention to the accompanying List of* EDUCATIONAL WORKS, *many of which have now attained a wide circulation.*

The Authors and Compilers are mostly scholars of repute, as well as of large experience in teaching.

Any notices of errors or defects in these publications will be gratefully received and acknowledged.

The Books can generally be procured through local Booksellers in town and country; but if at any time difficulty should arise, JAMES THORNTON *will feel obliged by direct communication on the subject.*

MISCELLANEOUS.

THE LATIN PRAYER BOOK OF CHARLES II.; or, an Account of the Liturgia of Dean Durel, together with a Reprint and Translation of the Catechism therein contained, with Collations, Annotations, and Appendices by the Rev. CHARLES MARSHALL, M.A., Chaplain to the Lord Mayor of London, 1849–1850; and WILLIAM W. MARSHALL, B.A., of the Inner Temple, late Scholar of Hertford College, Oxford. Demy 8vo. cloth, 10s. 6d. [*Just published.*

The Authors have been led to the present undertaking by a desire to attract more attention to the Latin Prayer Book of 1670, and they desire this for two reasons. Firstly, on account of the remarkable scarcity of the book itself. (In many of the most notable libraries no copy is to be found.) Secondly, because Durel's 'Liturgia' shows what the Revisers understood to be meant by the words which they retained and the words which they inserted; it shows the thought of the time as expressed by a contemporary and an authorised exponent.

CANONS OF THE SECOND COUNCIL OF ORANGE, A.D. 529. With an Introduction, Translation, and Notes. By the Rev. F. H. WOODS, M.A., Fellow of St. John's College, Oxford. Crown 8vo. 2s. [*Just published.*

An UNDERGRADUATE'S TRIP to ITALY and ATTICA in the WINTER of 1880-1. By J. L. THOMAS, Balliol College, Oxford. Crown 8vo. 5s.

THE LIVES AND LETTERS OF GIFFORD AND BUNYAN. By the Rev. T. A. BLYTH, Queen's College, Oxford. [*In preparation.*

CLASSICAL.

The **NICOMACHEAN ETHICS of ARISTOTLE.** Books I.–IV. and Book X. Chap. 6 to 9, being the portion required in the Oxford Pass School, with Notes, &c. for the use of Passmen. By E. L. HAWKINS, M.A., late Postmaster of Merton College. Demy 8vo. cloth, 8s. 6d. Interleaved with writing paper, 10s. 6d.

The **POETICS of ARISTOTLE.** The Text after Vahlen, with an Introduction, a New Translation, Explanatory and Critical Notes, and an Appendix on the Greek Drama. [*In preparation.*

JAMES THORNTON, 33 HIGH STREET, OXFORD.

CLASSICAL—*continued.*

DEMOSTHENES on the CROWN. The Text after BAITER. With an Introduction, a New Translation, Notes, and Indices. By FRANCIS P. SIMPSON, B.A., Balliol College, Craven Scholar, 1877. Demy 8vo. cloth, 10s. 6d. *[Just published.*

FROM THE PREFACE.—Several of the Notes—which I have tried to make as concise as possible—may appear unnecessary to a scholar; but they have been inserted for the practical reason that the obstacles they should remove have been felt by some of the many pupils with whom I have read this speech.

The main difficulty which Demosthenes presents to the student lies in the close logical connection of his arguments; and most commentaries consist largely of translation or paraphrase. Paraphrase is dangerous, as it may lead a novice to a belief that he quite understands a piece of Latin or Greek, when he is some way from doing so. I have, therefore, taken the bull by the horns, and have given a continuous rendering, as close as I could decently make it. Its aim is purely commentatorial—to save its weight in notes. It is intended to show what Demosthenes said, but not how well he said it. And, I may say, I believe that every lecturer and tutor in Oxford will admit that an undergraduate, or sixth-form boy, cannot get full value out of reading the De Corona without such help.

In Introduction I. will be found a sketch of Athenian history, as far as is necessary for the thorough understanding of this Oration. In Introduction II. a precis of the oration of Aeschines, as well as of that of Demosthenes, is prefixed to a brief analysis of the two speeches considered as an attack and a defence.

A SYNOPSIS of LIVY'S HISTORY of the SECOND PUNIC WAR. Books XXI.-XXIV. With Appendices, Notes, Maps, and Plans. By J. B. WORCESTER, M.A. Second Edition. Fcp. 8vo. cloth, 2s. 6d.

A SYNOPSIS and SUMMARY of the ANNALS of TACITUS. Books I.-VI. With Introduction, Notes and Indexes. By G. W. GENT, B.A. Crown 8vo. cloth, 3s. 6d.

A SYNOPSIS and SUMMARY of the REPUBLIC of PLATO. With a Prefatory Excursus upon the Platonic Philosophy, and Short Notes. By GEORGE WILLIAM GENT, B.A. *[Preparing.*

A FEW NOTES on the ANNALS of TACITUS. Books I. to IV. For Passmen. Crown 8vo. *[In the press.*

TRANSLATIONS.

The AGAMEMNON of ÆSCHYLUS. A new Prose Translation. Crown 8vo. cloth limp, 2s.

The NICOMACHEAN ETHICS of ARISTOTLE. A New Translation, with an Introduction, a Marginal Analysis, and Explanatory Notes. By D. P. CHASE, M.A., Fellow of Oriel College, and Principal of St. Mary Hall, Oxford. Fourth Edition, revised. Crown 8vo. cloth, 4s. 6d.

TRANSLATIONS—*continued.*

ARISTOTLE'S ORGANON : Translations from the Organon of Aristotle, comprising those Sections of Mr. Magrath's Selections required for Honour Moderations. By WALTER SMITH, New College, and ALLAN G. SUMNER GIBSON, Scholar of Corpus Christi College, Oxford. Crown 8vo. 2s. 6d

The ELEMENTS of ARISTOTLE'S LOGIC, following the order of Trendelenburg, with Introduction, English Translation, and Notes. By THOMAS CASE, M.A., Tutor of Corpus Christi College, and sometime Fellow of Brasenose College. *[Preparing.*

The PHILIPPIC ORATIONS of CICERO. A New Translation. By the Rev. JOHN RICHARD KING, M.A., Fellow and Tutor of Oriel College, Oxford. Crown 8vo. cloth, 4s. 6d.

The FIRST and SECOND PHILIPPIC ORATIONS of CICERO. A New Translation. By JOHN R. KING, M.A. Second Edition. Crown 8vo. 1s. 6d.

The SPEECH of CICERO for CLUENTIUS. Translated into English, with an Introduction and Notes. By W. PETERSON, M.A., late Scholar of Corpus Christi College, Oxford; Assistant to the Professor of Humanity in the University of Edinburgh. Crown 8vo. cloth, 3s. 6d. *[Just published.*

LIVY'S HISTORY of ROME. The Fifth, Sixth, and Seventh Books. A Literal Translation from the Text of MADVIG, with Historical Introductions, Summary to each Book, and Explanatory Notes. By a First Classman. Crown 8vo. 4s. 6d.

The MENO of PLATO. A New Translation, with Introduction and Explanatory Notes, for the use of Students. Crown 8vo. cloth limp, 1s. 6d.

PLUTARCH'S LIVES of the GRACCHI. Translated from the Text of Sintenis, with Introduction, Marginal Analysis, and Appendices. By W. W. MARSHALL, B.A., late Scholar of Hertford College. Crown 8vo. paper covers, 1s. 6d., or cloth, 2s.

The ÆNEID of VIRGIL. Books I. to IV. Translated into English Prose. By T. CLAYTON, M.A. Crown 8vo. cloth, 2s.

The ÆNEID of VIRGIL. A new Prose Translation. By THOMAS CLAYTON, M.A., Trinity College, Oxford. *[In preparation.*

JAMES THORNTON, 33 HIGH STREET, OXFORD.

CLASS BOOKS.

MELETEMATA; or, SELECT LATIN PASSAGES IN PROSE AND VERSE FOR UNPREPARED TRANSLATION. Arranged by the Rev. F. J. F. GANTILLON, M.A., sometime Scholar of St. John's College, Cambridge, Classical Master in Cheltenham College. Crown 8vo. cloth, 4s. 6d.

The object of this volume is to furnish a collection of about 250 passages, graduated in difficulty, and adapted to the various Examinations in which 'Unprepared Translation' finds a place.

'The work is nicely got up, and is altogether the best of the kind with which we are acquainted.'—THE SCHOOLMASTER, *December* 3, 1881.

'We find this collection to be very judiciously made, and think it one of the best which has yet been published.'—EDUCATIONAL TIMES, *April* 1, 1881.

MELETEMATA GRÆCA; being a Selection of Passages, Prose and Verse, for unprepared Translation. By the Rev. P. J. F. GANTILLON, M.A. *[In the press.*

Forming a Companion Volume to the above.

SELECTED PIECES for TRANSLATION into LATIN PROSE. Selected and arranged by the Rev. H. C. OGLE, M.A. Head Master of Magdalen College School, and T. CLAYTON, M.A. Crown 8vo. cloth, 4s. 6d.

This selection is intended for the use of the highest forms in Schools and for University Students for Honour Examinations, for whom it was felt that a small and compact book would be most serviceable.

'The selection has been made with much care and the passages which we have more particularly examined are very appropriate for translation.'

SCHOOL GUARDIAN, *June* 7, 1879.

LATIN and GREEK VERSIONS of some of the SELECTED PIECES for TRANSLATION. Collected and arranged by the Rev. H. C. OGLE, M.A., Head Master of Magdalen College School; and THOMAS CLAYTON, M.A., Trinity College, Oxford. Crown 8vo. 5s. *[Just ready.*

This Key is for the use of Tutors only, and is issued on the understanding that it does not get into the hands of any pupil.

For the convenience of Schoolmasters and Tutors these Versions are also issued in another form, viz on separate leaves ready for distribution to pupils, thereby saving the necessity of dictating or copying. They are done up in packets of twenty-five each, and not less than twenty-five sets (=76 packets) can be supplied at a time. Price—Thirty-five Shillings net.

DAMON; or, The ART of GREEK IAMBIC MAKING. By the Rev. J. HERBERT WILLIAMS, M.A., Composition Master in S. Nicholas College, Lancing; late Demy of Magdalen College. Fcp. 8vo. 1s. 6d.

This small treatise claims as its merit that it really teaches Greek Iambic writing on a system, and this system is based on no arbitrary analysis of the Iambic line, but on the way in which the scholar practically regards it in making verses himself.

A Key, for Tutors only. Fcp. 8vo. cloth, 3s. 6d.

SHORT TABLES and NOTES on GREEK and LATIN GRAMMAR. By W. E. W. COLLINS, M.A., Jesus College. Crown 8vo. cloth, 2s.

ARS SCRIBENDI LATINE; or, Aids to Latin Prose Composition. In the Form of an Analysis of Latin Idioms. By B. A. EDWARDS, B.A., late Scholar of Jesus College, Oxford. Crown 8vo. 1s.

OUTLINES of CHEMICAL THEORY. By FREDERICK FINNIS GRENSTED, B.A., University College. [*In preparation.*

ARITHMETIC FOR SCHOOLS. Based on principles of Cause and Effect. By the Rev. FREDERICK SPARKS, M.A., Mathematical Master, the High School, Plymouth, and late Lecturer of Worcester College, Oxford. [*In preparation.*

ALGEBRAICAL QUESTIONS AND EXERCISES. For the Use of Candidates for Matriculation, Responsions, and First Public Examinations, and the Oxford and Cambridge Local and Certificate Examinations. Crown 8vo. 2s.

ARITHMETICAL QUESTIONS AND EXERCISES. For the Use of Candidates for Matriculation, Responsions, and First Public Examinations, and the Oxford and Cambridge Local and Certificate Examinations. Crown 8vo. 1s. 6d.

QUESTIONS AND EXERCISES IN ADVANCED LOGIC. For the Use of Candidates for the Honour Moderation Schools. Crown 8vo. 1s. 6d.

The RUDIMENTS of LOGIC, with Tables and Examples. By F. E. WEATHERLY, M.A. Fcp. 8vo. cloth limp, 1s. 6d.
'Here is everything needful for a beginner.'—EDUCATIONAL TIMES.
'Is a clever condensation of first principles.'—SCHOOL GUARDIAN.

A FEW NOTES on the GOSPELS. By W. E. W. COLLINS, M.A., Jesus College. New Edition. Crown 8vo. paper covers, 1s. 6d.

PALÆSTRA OXONIENSIS.

The object of this Series is to furnish Exercises and Test Papers for Candidates preparing for the various Examinations at our Public School and Universities.

QUESTIONS and EXERCISES for MATRICULATION and RESPONSIONS. CONTENTS: (1) Grammatical Questions in Greek and Latin; (2) Materials for Latin Prose; (3) Questions on Authors. Sixth Edition. Crown 8vo. cloth, 3s. 6d.

PALÆSTRA OXONIENSIS—*continued.*

QUESTIONS and EXERCISES for CLASSICAL SCHOLAR-
SHIPS. CONTENTS: (1) Critical Grammar Questions in Greek and
Latin; (2) Unseen passages for translation. Adapted to the Oxford
and Cambridge Schools Certificate and the Oxford First Public
Examinations. Second Edition, corrected and enlarged. Crown
8vo. cloth, 3s. 6d.
Elucidations to the Critical Questions, with Key to the Unseen Passages,
in preparation.

QUESTIONS and EXERCISES for CLASSICAL SCHOLAR-
SHIPS. Second Division. CONTENTS: (1) Historical and General
Questions; (2) Subjects for English Essays. Crown 8vo. cloth,
3s. 6d.

QUESTIONS and EXERCISES in ELEMENTARY MATHE-
MATICS. CONTENTS: (1) Arithmetic; (2) Algebra; (3) Euclid.
Third Edition, enlarged. Adapted to Matriculation, Responsions,
and First Public Examinations, and the Oxford and Cambridge
Local and Certificate Examinations. Crown 8vo. cloth, 3s. 6d. With
ANSWERS, 5s. The ANSWERS separately, paper covers, 1s. 6d.

QUESTIONS and EXERCISES in ELEMENTARY LOGIC,
DEDUCTIVE and INDUCTIVE; with Index of Logical Terms.
Crown 8vo. cloth. (New Edition in the press.)

QUESTIONS and EXERCISES in RUDIMENTARY DI-
VINITY. CONTENTS: (1) Old Testament; (2) New Testament;
(3) The Thirty-Nine Articles; (4) Greek Passages for Translation.
Adapted to the Oxford Pass and the Oxford and Cambridge Certificate Examinations. Second Edition. Crown 8vo. cloth, 3s. 6d.

ELEMENTARY QUESTIONS on the LAW of PROPERTY,
REAL and PERSONAL. Supplemented by Advanced Questions on
the Law of Contracts. With Copious References throughout, and
an Index of Legal Terms. Crown 8vo. cloth, 3s. 6d.

QUESTIONS and EXERCISES in POLITICAL ECONOMY,
with References to Adam Smith, Ricardo, John Stuart Mill, Fawcett,
J. E. Thorold Rogers, Bonamy Price, Twiss, Senior, and others.
Crown 8vo. cloth, 3s. 6d.

LAW AND POLITICAL ECONOMY.

THOMAS HOBBES, of MALMESBURY, LEVIATHAN
or, the Matter, Forme, and Power of a Commonwealth. A New
Reprint. With a facsimile of the original fine engraved Title.
Medium 8vo. cloth, 12s. 6d. A small edition of 250 copies only,
on Dutch hand-made paper, medium 8vo. 18s.
Students' Edition, crown 8vo. cloth 8s. 6d.   [*Just published.*

REMARKS on the USE and ABUSE of SOME POLITICAL
TERMS. By the late Right Hon. Sir GEORGE CORNEWALL LEWIS,
Bart., sometime Student of Christ Church, Oxford. A New Edition,
with Notes and Appendix. By Sir ROLAND KNYVET WILSON, Bart.,
M.A., Barrister-at-Law; late Fellow of King's College, Cambridge;
Author of 'History of Modern English Law.' Crown 8vo. 6s.

FROM THE EDITOR'S PREFACE.

'The value of the book for educational purposes consists not so much
in its positive results, as in the fact that it opens a vein of thought which
the student may usefully follow out to any extent for himself, and that it
affords an instructive example of a thoughtful, scientific, and in the best
sense academical style of treating political questions.

'With regard to my own annotations, the object which I have chiefly
kept in view has been to direct attention to such later writings as have
expressly undertaken to fix the scientific meaning of the political terms
here discussed, and above all "Austin's Lectures on Jurisprudence," to
which the present work may be considered as a kind of companion volume.'

QUESTIONS and EXERCISES in POLITICAL ECONOMY,
with References to Adam Smith, Ricardo, John Stuart Mill, Fawcett,
Thorold Rogers, Bonamy Price, Twiss, Senior, Macleod, and others.
Adapted to the Oxford Pass and Honour and the Cambridge Ordinary
B.A. Examinations. Arranged and edited by W. P. EMERTON, M.A.,
B.C.L., Christ Church, Oxford. Crown 8vo. cloth, 3s. 6d.

This volume consists of Questions mainly taken from various Examination Papers with references in the case of the easier questions, and hints,
and in some cases formal statements of the arguments *pro* and *con.* to the
more difficult questions. There are also two Appendixes on the debated
questions—'Is Political Economy a Science?' and 'Is Political Economy
Selfish?'

An ABRIDGMENT of ADAM SMITH'S INQUIRY into the
NATURE and CAUSES of the WEALTH of NATIONS. By
W. P. EMERTON, M.A., B.C.L. Crown 8vo. cloth, 6s.

This work (based on Jeremiah Joyce's Abridgment) originally appeared
in two parts and is now republished after careful revision, with Additional
Notes, Appendices, and a Complete Index.
The two Parts can still be had separately. Part I. Books I. and II. 3s. 6d.
Part II. Books III., IV. and V. 3s. 6d.

LAW AND POLITICAL ECONOMY—*continued.*

OUTLINES of JURISPRUDENCE. For the Use of Students. By B. R. Wise, late Scholar of Queen's College, Oxford; Oxford Cobden Prizeman, 1878. Crown 8vo. cloth, 5s. [*Now ready.*

This book is intended to be a critical and explanatory commentary upon the Jurisprudence text-books in common use; and it endeavours to present a precise and coherent view of all the topics upon which these touch.

OUTLINES of ENGLISH CONSTITUTIONAL HISTORY. By Britiffe Constable Skottowe, B.A., late Scholar of New College, Oxford. Crown 8vo. cloth, 3s. 6d.

The object of this book is to assist beginners in reading Constitutional History by arranging in order outlines of the growth of the most important Institutions.

An ANALYSIS of the ENGLISH LAW of REAL PRO-PERTY, chiefly from Blackstone's Commentary, with Tables and Indexes. By Gordon Campbell, M.A., Author of 'An Analysis of Austin's Lectures on Jurisprudence,' and of 'A Compendium of Roman Law.' Crown 8vo. cloth, 3s. 6d.

An ANALYSIS of JUSTINIAN'S INSTITUTES of ROMAN LAW, with Tables. [*In preparation.*

A CHRONOLOGICAL SUMMARY of the CHIEF REAL PROPERTY STATUTES, with their more important Provisions. For the Use of Law Students. By P. F. Aldred, M.A., B.C.L. Crown 8vo. 2s.

ELEMENTARY QUESTIONS on the LAW of PROPERTY, REAL and PERSONAL. Supplemented by Advanced Questions on the Law of Contracts. With Copious References throughout, and an Index of Legal Terms. Crown 8vo. cloth, 3s. 6d.

The SPECIAL STATUTES required by Candidates for the School of Jurisprudence at Oxford. Fcp. 8vo. sewed, 2s. 6d. With brief Notes and Translations by a B.C.L. Cloth, 5s.

OXFORD STUDY GUIDES.

A SERIES OF HANDBOOKS TO EXAMINATIONS.

Edited by F. S. PULLING, M.A., Exeter College.

THE object of this Series is to guide Students in their reading for the different examinations. The amount of time wasted at present, simply through ignorance of the way to read, is so great that the Editor and Authors feel convinced of the necessity for some such handbooks, and they trust that these Guides will at least do something to prevent in the future the misapplication of so much industry.

Each volume will be confined to one branch of study, and will include an account of the various Scholarships and Prizes offered by the University or the Colleges in its department; and will be undertaken by a writer whose experience qualifies him to speak with authority on the subject.

The books will contain extracts from the University Statutes relating to the Examinations, with an attempt to explain them as they exist, and advice as to what to read and how to read ; how to prepare subjects for examination, and how to answer papers ; a few specimen questions, extracts from the Regulations of the Board of Studies, and a list of books.

THEOLOGY. By the Rev. F. H. Woods, M.A., Fellow of St. John's College. Crown 8vo. cloth, 2s. 6d. [*Ready.*

JAMES THORNTON, 38 HIGH STREET, OXFORD. 11

OXFORD STUDY GUIDES—*continued.*

ENTRANCE CLASSICAL SCHOLARSHIPS. By S. H. Jeyes, B.A.,
Classical Lecturer at University College, and late Scholar of Trinity
College. Crown 8vo. cloth, 2*s.* 6*d.* [*Ready.*

'It is quite refreshing to find a guide to an examination that so thoroughly discourages cram.'—School Guardian, *June* 20, 1881.

'This is a smart book, and a useful comment on the present method of awarding scholarships. There is a certain frank cynicism in much of the advice, as when Mr. Jeyes remarks, It is no good wearing out your trousers in a study chair, if you do not set your brains to work;" or that it "is quite useless to play at hide-and-seek with examiners who are familiar with every turn and twist in the game;" and there seems little doubt that a clever boy, coached by him on his method, would get a scholarship.'—Spectator, *Aug.* 27, 1881.

Mr. Jeyes has provided parents and teachers with an excellent manual by which to guide their sons or pupils in preparing for University Scholarships...... He gives directions as to the best way of preparing for the different sorts of papers...... and also for the best way of tackling with the paper when confronted with it in actual examination. The observations are of the most practical kind...... The book is well done, and ought to be useful.'—The Academy, *June* 18, 1881.

HONOUR CLASSICAL MODERATIONS. By L. R. Farnell, B.A.,
Fellow of Exeter College. Crown 8vo. cloth, 2*s.* 6*d.* [*Ready.*

LITERÆ HUMANIORES. By E. B. Iwan-Müller, B.A., New College.
[*Shortly.*

MODERN HISTORY. By F. S. Pulling, M.A., Exeter College. [*Shortly.*

NATURAL SCIENCE. By E. B. Poulton, M.A., Keble College. [*Shortly.*

JURISPRUDENCE and CIVIL LAW. By W. P. Emerton, M.A.,
B.C.L., Christ Church. [*In preparation.*

MATHEMATICS.—*To be arranged for.*

CPSIA information can be obtained
at www.ICGtesting.com
Printed in the USA
LVHW081304241020
669716LV00047B/3226